CYCLING
GETTING STARTED

CYCLING
GETTING STARTED

ALL YOU NEED TO KNOW ABOUT CYCLING BASICS, FROM CHOOSING THE
RIGHT BIKE TO MOUNTAIN BIKING AND TOURING, WITH 245 PHOTOGRAPHS

ADVICE ON SAFETY, CLOTHING AND EQUIPMENT, MAINTENANCE AND REPAIR,
SO YOU CAN MAKE THE MOST OF YOUR BIKE FOR COMMUTING OR LEISURE

EDWARD PICKERING

HERMES
HOUSE

This edition is published by Hermes House,
an imprint of Anness Publishing Ltd, Blaby Road, Wigston,
Leicestershire LE18 4SE

Email: info@anness.com

Web: www.hermeshouse.com; www.annesspublishing.com

If you like the images in this book and would like to investigate using them for publishing, promotions or advertising,
please visit our website www.practicalpictures.com for more information.

Publisher: Joanna Lorenz
Project Editor: Anne Hildyard
Photographers: Phil O'Connor and Geoff Waugh
Designer: Steve West
Jacket Design: Nigel Partridge
Production Controller: Christine Ni

PUBLISHER'S NOTE
Although the advice and information in this book are believed to be accurate and true at the time of going to press, neither
the authors nor the publisher can accept any legal responsibility or liability for any errors or omissions that may be made nor
for any inaccuracies nor for any harm or injury that comes about from following instructions or advice in this book. You are
advised to consult your doctor before commencing a new exercise programme.

A CIP catalogue record for this book is available from the British Library.

Previously published as part of a larger volume, *The Illustrated Practical Encyclopedia of Cycling*

CONTENTS

Introduction

The bicycle symbolizes freedom, mobility, independence and self-sufficiency. It is far more than a mode of transport – it is a toy, a means to lifelong health and fitness, and the most environmentally friendly and efficient way of getting from A to B.

This book will explain everything you need to know to make the most of your cycling experience, whether you are a beginner or an expert, a road rider or a mountain biker.

The book starts with riding for pleasure and for practical purposes, taking you through the history of the development of bikes, before explaining the basic skills you need to get started. We'll describe leisure cycling, commuting, cycling for the family and how to get your children involved. For the more adventurous, the book covers the ultimate in leisure cycling – touring. We'll explain how you can make your bike part of your holiday, and advise you on what to take and where to go. There is a section on bike technology in which we take your bike apart and explain how the moving parts work, and how to maintain them in perfect working order.

Farther on, find out how to use your bike to get fitter. We'll look at the best places in the world to enjoy mountain biking. We'll also take a look at the world's greatest bike races. Find out about off-road racing, including cross-country mountain bike racing and cyclo-cross, as well as track racing. Lastly, we look at advanced training methods, and dealing with injuries.

Above: In Amsterdam, cycling is a popular way to get around, and there are bicycles on every street.

Why cycle?

The beauty of cycling is that you can participate at any level, be it for practical reasons such as commuting, to compete seriously, or simply just for fun. For many

Below: Off-road biking has exploded in popularity since the first mountain bikes became available in the late 1980s.

Above: The ultimate achievement in road cycling – Tom Boonen wins a stage of the Tour de France in 2007.

Left: Many children's first experience of cycling comes through BMXing, which enables them to develop riding skills, confidence and agility.

people, the bicycle is the first step to independence and exploration. On foot, children can explore to the end of the road and perhaps a little way beyond, but on a bike, their freedom grows exponentially. Millions, perhaps billions of children around the world have grown up with their bike as their companion. Many leave the bike behind when they enter adulthood, but increasingly, we are seeing bicycles with fresh eyes. More and more adults are riding for fun, for fitness or purely for practical reasons.

Urban cycling

Cities around the world are following the lead of European capitals such as Amsterdam and incorporating bike lanes into their transport policy and many provide bikes to hire, so there is no

need to buy your own bike. There is no cheaper, cleaner, greener method of getting around town. Bikes are also fast. In competition with a car in a gridlocked city, the bike wins every time.

However, speed is not always of the essence. People ride bikes mainly for fun. With the invention of the BMX and its popularization in the 1980s, and the explosion of interest in mountain biking in the 1990s, cycling has been one of the fastest-growing leisure activities in the Western world.

As we become more adventurous in our choice of holiday, the bike has become a popular method of transport. It is not enough to go touring at home, people are organizing long cycling tours all over Europe and America, and farther afield in Asia and Africa.

One of the most effective methods of keeping fit is cycling. If you cycle, you are exercising, and by doing it you will look better and become fitter, healthier and happier.

HISTORY AND DEVELOPMENT

It is remarkable how little the basic design of the bicycle has changed since its invention in the 19th century. Although the overall look – two wheels, a frame, handlebars and saddle – has been constant, there has still been significant evolution. Once pneumatic tyres and efficient drivetrains had been invented, the bicycle revolutionized personal transport. From the earliest 'running machines', to the lightweight, aerodynamic carbon-fibre racing bike, bicycles have come a long way.

Above: A hobby horse from the early 19th century.
Left: An 'ordinary' bicycle, commonly known as a 'penny farthing'.

In the Beginning

In the past, most people had little choice but to walk everywhere. The invention of the bicycle provided the means for individuals to travel farther than ever before, making it the first real widespread mode of transport among the public.

Claims have been made that Leonardo da Vinci, among others, invented the bicycle, but the first reliable evidence for self-propelled two-wheeled transport comes from 1817.

Baron Karl Drais von Sauerbronn, a civil servant from Baden, Germany, invented a steerable two-wheeled device initially named the 'Draisine', after its maker. More popularly known as a running machine, or hobby horse, the Draisine was made of a wooden frame attached to two wheels. Propulsion was basic – without pedals or a drivetrain, the rider had to push the Draisine along using his feet on the ground. Following an exhibition in Paris in April 1818, Draisines enjoyed a flurry of popularity among the wealthy, but they were impractical on all but the smoothest of road surfaces.

Treadle power

Scottish blacksmith Kirkpatrick Macmillan invented a treadle-driven bicycle in 1839, the first attempt at a modern propulsion system. Pedals were attached to two rods, which connected to the back wheel and transmitted movement in a way similar to a steam train. The energy transmission was very inefficient, but Macmillan's bicycle was reportedly capable of sustaining low speeds, as fast as 8 miles per hour, for long distances. Bicycle design took a great leap forward in 1861, when Frenchman Pierre Michaux took Drais's

Above: Baron Karl Drais von Sauerbronn and his 'Draisine' bicycle, which was propelled by the feet.

design and added pedals and cranks directly to the front wheel. Michaux's bicycle, or velocipede (which means 'fast foot' in French), was developed into what we now know as penny farthings, or 'ordinary' bikes.

The invention of gearing was a long way off, therefore the only way to increase speed was to make the driving wheel, usually the front one, larger in diameter. As one pedal revolution was equal to one rotation of the wheel, the larger the circumference, the faster the bike would travel through one revolution of the pedal.

Left: In the mid-1800s, treadle-driven bicycles made it possible to ride for long distances at low speed.

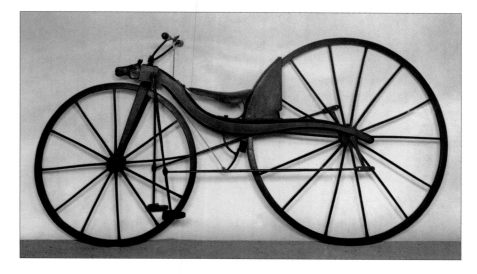

Timeline

1817 Baron Karl Drais von Sauerbronn invents the running machine, a wooden frame on two wheels, with steering ability. Propulsion came from the rider pushing himself along using his feet on the ground.
1839 Kirkpatrick Macmillan builds a bicycle with the rear wheel powered by treadles.
1861 Pierre Michaux makes the first bicycle with pedals and cranks.
1869 Solid rubber tyres mounted on steel rims are introduced in a new machine, which is the first to be patented under the modern name 'bicycle'.
1870s Penny farthings are popularized.

1885 The safety bicycle, with a chain-driven back wheel, is invented by James Starley.
1888 John Boyd Dunlop develops the pneumatic tyre.
1899 Production of bicycles in America reaches one million units per year.
1903 The first Tour de France takes place.
1927 Quick-release wheels are invented by Tullio Campagnolo.
1933 Derailleur gears are developed.
1960s BMXs originate in California. Through the 1970s they increase in popularity.
1970s Mountain biking starts, also in California, with modified cruiser bikes

ridden downhill and off-road. They become extremely popular in the 1980s and 1990s.
1985 Clipless racing pedals invented by French company Look.
1990 Off-road clipless pedals are developed.
1990 Suspension forks introduced to mass-marketed mountain bikes.
1992 Full suspension bikes are developed.
1996 Mountain biking appears in the Olympic Games.
1999 American Lance Armstrong wins his first Tour de France; this event leads to widespread popularity of bike racing outside Europe.

Painful progress

The concept of the pedal-driven bicycle was revolutionary, but bikes at this time were not built for comfort. Frames were made of heavy steel, unlike modern frames, which use lightweight tubing, and wheels were made of wood. Tyres were simply a thin strip of metal wrapped around the wheel – combined with the cobbled streets of the era, the invariably bumpy ride led to the new machines being called 'boneshakers'. It was not until 1869 that solid rubber tyres were developed, although these were scarcely less harsh than the metal strips.

The high centre of gravity and uneven weight distribution meant that accidents were common. If the huge front wheel of a penny farthing hit an obstacle, the rider, with legs trapped beneath the handlebars, was catapulted forward at the same speed as he had previously been travelling – with the direst of consequences. This way of falling became known as 'coming a cropper'. Nevertheless, during the 1870s, penny farthings were a popular means of getting around.

Right: 'Ordinary' bicycles first became popular during the 1870s. The larger the front wheel, the faster it became possible to ride.

Development of the Modern Bicycle

Following the early and bumpy start of bicycle riding, developments in engineering and technology during the late 19th century led to radical improvements in bike design. Similar-sized wheels made the bicycle much easier to ride.

Ordinary bikes were popular for leisure riding through the 1870s, mainly among young middle- and upper-class men who performed feats of reckless derring-do. The danger inherent in riding ordinaries meant that bicycles were still some way from becoming a universal transport device. However, the bicycle was on the cusp of several significant developments, which would see a radical evolution in efficiency over the next 120 years.

The invention of the 'safety bicycle' by James Starley in 1885 revolutionized bicycle design. Technological developments meant that by 1885 metals had become stronger, and it was possible to make a chain that was light enough to be incorporated into a bicycle drivetrain. Starley's Rover bicycle was the first to look like a modern model, with more similar-sized wheels, a diamond-shaped frame, and a chain connecting the pedals with the back wheel. Its weight distribution was better than that of the ordinary, and braking was improved. With the chain and sprocket drivetrain, gearing could be adjusted to make propulsion vastly more efficient.

Rubber tyres

The Rover was still hard work to ride until James Dunlop invented the pneumatic rubber tyre in 1888. The new design used hollow tyres filled with air to cushion the bumps on the roads and offered a more comfortable, faster and safer ride. At the same time, a seat tube was added to the standard frame design, to strengthen it, and this classic 'double triangle diamond' frame shape has survived to the 21st century.

The invention of freewheels, where the wheel can continue to turn while the sprocket stays still, made it possible for riders to coast down hills. Now that bikes were comfortable and fast, the 1890s saw the beginning of a

golden age for two-wheeled transport, which was interrupted by two World Wars, but which would last until the 1950s. Mass production reduced the cost of bicycles to a low level, making them accessible to the working classes.

Above: The advent of the bicycle was an important step on the road to independence for women in the early 20th century, as it was accessible to many who had previously been restricted to walking.

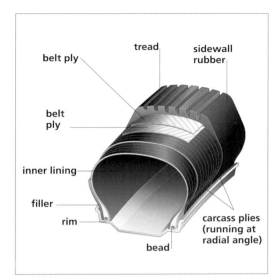

Above: A cross section of a pneumatic tyre, which revolutionized cycling by giving a faster, more comfortable ride.

In the USA alone, bicycle production reached an annual high of one million units by 1899. Women, still bound by Victorian concepts of modesty, would not think of riding an ordinary, but the safety bicycle let them ride without offending sensibilities. The new-found travelling freedom of the working classes and women made the bicycle into an almost universal tool. Suffragettes embraced two-wheel transport, with American civil rights leader Susan B. Anthony claiming that "the bicycle has done more for the emancipation of women than anything else in the world".

Meanwhile, in Europe, bike racing grew as a popular sport. Events like the Tour de France, which first ran in 1903, captured the public imagination. Into the 20th century, bikes grew in popularity and use. The pace of innovation in bicycle design slowed, until an Italian racing cyclist called Tullio Campagnolo made two significant developments during the 1920s and 1930s. The first was the quick-release wheel, which made disassembly much simpler. The second was the derailleur gear system, which is still seen on bikes today. Campagnolo's parallelogram-shaped derailleur allowed the chain to move between several sprockets on the back wheel, giving a wide range of gears so that the bikes could be easily ridden on hills, as well as along the flat.

The boom in car ownership ended the popularity of bicycles. After 1945, while car numbers grew, sales of bikes in Britain went from a pre-war peak of 1.6 million in 1935 to fewer than half a million in 1955. In the US, numbers dropped even more, but technological development continued. Utility bikes remained popular in Europe, while in the Far East, the bicycle was the main mode of transport. Racing bikes were made stronger, lighter and faster, and bikes now come with up to 33 gears.

Touring bikes were built to carry luggage and camping equipment. Bicycles started to go off-road, especially with the advent of BMX and mountain bikes, which saw the development of suspension systems for greater comfort. Efficiency was gained by the use of clipless pedals; shoes were attached to the pedals for propulsion, but would release in the event of an accident.

Sales rose again during the 1970s and 1980s. Today, with environmental concerns about the impact of driving, the bicycle stands on the cusp of another golden age.

Below: Racing bikes are among the most technologically advanced models available today.

Diversification

As technology developed, it became possible to diversify and to produce bicycles that could be ridden on rough terrain as well as on roads. This opened up opportunities for producing bikes for both leisure and sporting activities.

Until the 1970s, bicycles were functional, utilitarian and serious. Utility bikes were used for commuting and shopping, touring bikes were the ultimate in self-sufficiency and practicality, and racing bikes were honed down for speed and efficiency. In California, however, two inventions revolutionized the world of bicycles and laid the foundations for a boom in cycling as a leisure and adventure activity. The first was BMX (bicycle moto-cross), the second, mountain biking.

The rise of BMX

BMX developed out of an American craze for a Schwinn model called the Sting-Ray, which came on the market in 1963. The Sting-Ray had fat tyres on small 50cm (20in) wheels with a heavy-duty frame. By 1968, almost three-quarters of all bikes sold in the United States were Sting-Rays or similar models.

BMX, an abbreviation of 'bicycle moto-cross', came about when the opening sequence to motorcycling film *On Any Sunday* showed children racing

Above: This young BMX rider is appropriately kitted out with protective trousers and jacket, a helmet with a chin extension, visor, gloves and shoes.

Two wheels, two people

It wasn't long after bicycles were invented that creative minds made a logical leap – if a bike can carry one person, why not two? And so tandems were invented. The first try was two bicycles welded together. But a patent was filed on 4 August 1891 by H. G. Barr and F.E. Peck for a two-man velocipede with one seat above each wheel and pedals on each axle. Modern tandems have a strong wheel and frame to bear the weight of two riders. They can be faster than a single bike, because they harness the power of two riders through a single drivetrain.

Left: This Spanish couple started a 10-year journey on their tandem in 2005, encompassing more than 80 different countries.

Above: A modern BMX; solid, durable with a single gear.

Above: This American cruiser is a bike that is aimed squarely at children.

Above: A heavy-duty mountain bike, a Stumpjumper, for off-road riding.

their Sting-Rays on a dirt track. Races sprang up around the country, and the bikes became more like moto-cross bikes, with knobbly tyres and crossbars on the handlebars. Through the 1970s the BMX craze took off, first in America, then in Europe, as the sport and bikes evolved a distinctive look. By 1975, BMXers had started freestyling in skateboarding parks in California, and performing complex jumps and tricks.

In the 1980s BMX hit mainstream culture, with top stunt riders and racers earning big money.

The US television channel ESPN sponsored a televised race series with a first-prize fund that reached more than $50,000. BMX peaked in the mid-1980s, but even now, more BMXs are sold in North America than any other kind of bike.

Mountain biking

In the 1970s and 1980s, a new and innovative form of cycling followed on the heels of the BMX craze. This was to be the start of mountain biking. Its roots are obscured somewhat but it is known that a group of riders in Marin County, California, started customizing their bikes with fatter tyres and extremely efficient brakes.

In the 1970s, the first downhill race took place when riders raced down a hill known as Repack Road. Repack descended 400m in 3km (1,300ft in 2 miles), and the races grew in size, then spread to other locations. In 1977 the first purpose-built mountain bike became available, and the mainstream media began to recognize a new craze. In 1982, the first mass-produced mountain bike was developed – the Specialized Stumpjumper – and sales boomed worldwide. Technology continued to refine the mountain bike, with suspension forks, full-suspension bikes and disc brakes.

Mountain biking is now one of the biggest branches of cycling for sport and leisure in the United States and Europe.

Below: The Schwinn Sting-Ray was the first bike aimed at the youth market.

Cycling as a Sport

As soon as bicycles had evolved enough to go fast, people started racing them. Pierre Michaux's velocipede was invented in 1861, and within 10 years the first recorded race had taken place. The popularity of that event confirmed bicycle racing as a sport.

In Saint-Cloud Park, in Paris, on 31 May 1869, the first velocipede race took place – a 1,200m (0.75 mile) event, with James Moore, an expatriate English doctor, taking first place. Since 1,200m was well below the distance potentially covered by a bicycle in one day, it wasn't long before races were being run between separate towns. The inaugural Paris–Rouen race, also in 1869, covered 122km (76 miles). Moore won that race, too. Considering that pneumatic tyres were yet to be invented, then the average speed of 11kph (7mph) recorded by Moore becomes even more impressive.

Bicycle racing became more and more popular in the last decade of the 19th century, with massed-start races drawing huge crowds and competitors from all over Europe. Place-to-place events were the biggest draw, and distance was no object to the organizers of these events. Bordeaux–Paris, raced for the first time in 1891, covered a gruelling 600km (373 miles). Another Englishman, George Pilkington-Mills, raced through the night to win the race in just over 24 hours. Although another Briton, Arthur Linton, won five years later, only one more would win the race before the final running of the event in 1988 – Tom Simpson in 1963. The same year saw the even longer Paris–Brest–Paris event, which covered 1,200km (745 miles) across northern France, and was won in 71 hours by Frenchman Charles Terront. This event still exists as a four-yearly endurance test for amateur cyclists.

Professional races

The oldest professional race that is still running on an annual basis is the Liège–Bastogne–Liège Classic, which took place in Belgium for the first time in 1892, and was won for three years in a row by the Belgian cyclist Leon Houa.

Above: Fausto Coppi, one of the first great champions of road racing. Coppi captured the heart of post-war Italy when he won the Tour of Italy in 1955.

Liège–Bastogne–Liège was run only five more times before 1919, but it then became an annual fixture and remains one of the most important bike races in the world.

The most renowned one-day classic is the Paris–Roubaix race, which first took place in 1896. To this day, it still uses the old cobbled forest roads of industrial northern France, and has the nickname the 'Hell of the North'. Racing over cobbled roads is a different proposition from racing on smooth tarmac – Paris–Roubaix is a race that tests cyclists to their limits.

At the turn of the 20th century, bike races were still organized on a place-to-place basis, but a stroke of marketing genius in November 1902 changed the nature of bike racing forever.

Henri Desgrange, a journalist for French newspaper *L'Auto*, came up with

Left: The Tour de France in 1964, going along a scenic but challenging part of the route.

the idea of a bike race around France for July 1903 – not just from one place to another, but around the entire country – as a means of promoting the newspaper. The distance – 2,414km (1,500 miles) – was massive, so Desgrange split the race up into six stages, starting in Paris, then heading to Lyon, Marseille, Toulouse, Bordeaux and Nantes before returning to Paris. The stages might have been designed to break up the race, but the distances were still huge – the longest stage, between Nantes and Paris, was 471km (292 miles). The winner of the first race was Frenchman Maurice Garin, who won the substantial sum of 20,000 francs for his efforts.

L'Auto provided daily coverage of the race, and boosted circulation from 25,000 copies to 65,000 in the space of a few weeks. The positive publicity led Desgrange to make the Tour an annual event and it quickly became, and remains, the biggest and most famous bike race in the world.

Above: Eddy Merckx, winning his first Tour de France in 1969. He set a record that remains unbroken.

Below: Crowds line a mountainous stretch of the road to see the competitors pass in the 1949 Tour de France.

The world stage

In the early part of the 20th century, more and more stage races sprang up around Europe. The Giro d'Italia, or Tour of Italy, which is generally considered to be the second most important Grand Tour after the Tour de France, was started in 1909, while the Vuelta a Espana, Spain's version, followed suit in 1935. Meanwhile, important one-day races, such as the Tour of Lombardy and Milan–San Remo in Italy, and the Tour of Flanders in Belgium, became established.

As the races grew in size, the riders themselves became famous. Before and after World War II, the rivalry between two Italian riders, Gino Bartali and Fausto Coppi, divided the nation.

Bartali, a staunch Catholic with a modest and conservative disposition, attracted older fans, while the secular Coppi, who created a scandal by divorcing his wife – an unpopular move in religious Italy – was identified with by younger, more progressive Italians. The two went head to head in the 1949 Giro d'Italia, and Coppi thrashed his older rival.

Coppi's 1952 Tour de France win is renowned as being one of the best of all time. The organizers had introduced tough stages through the Pyrenees and

Alps since the 1910 race. But in 1952 they made another important development – the summit finish. With stages to ski resorts such as

Above: Eddy Merckx, shown in 1974 in Vouvray, Orléans, is held to be the best-ever racing cyclist.

Alpe d'Huez, the final kilometres were all uphill, which made the race even harder. Coppi won at Alpe d'Huez, which has become a regular fixture on the Tour, and dominated the race.

The first rider to win the Tour five times was Frenchman Jacques Anquetil, between 1957 and 1964, while his compatriot Bernard Hinault in the 1970s and 1980s and Spaniard Miguel Indurain in the 1990s also won five Tours. The two most famous multiple winners of the Tour were Belgian cycling star Eddy Merckx and American Lance Armstrong (see boxes).

Now, the Tour is a multi-million-euro affair that captures the attention of sport fans every summer. From humble beginnings in 1869, bike racing has become a global sport.

Right: Tom Boonen rides on cobbled roads in the Paris–Roubaix race in 2004.

Eddy Merckx

Belgian cyclist Eddy Merckx was the first international superstar of bicycle road racing. During a professional career spanning 13 years from 1965 to 1978, he won a record number of races – as many as 575, according to some – including five Tours de France.

Merckx's nickname was 'the Cannibal' – he had as insatiable an appetite for being the winner of bike races as Muhammad Ali had for winning boxing fights. His racing style was aggressive, and he would often attack a long way from the finish.

Early in his career, he took victories in prestigious one-day races like Milan–San Remo and Paris–Roubaix. He also won three world championships, a record equalled, but never beaten. To add to his five Tour de France wins, he also won five Tours of Italy (Giro d'Italia) and one Tour of Spain (Vuelta a

Espana) – no cyclist in history has come anywhere close to matching Merckx's 11 victories in Grand Tours.

But it was the Tour de France that defined Merckx's career. He won his first Tour in 1969, at his first attempt, and took his fifth and final win in 1974, equalling the record of five overall wins set by the Frenchman Jacques Anquetil.

Merckx's first Tour de France in 1969 was one of the most dominant victories in the history of the race. As well as winning the yellow jersey (awarded to the rider who covers the course in the best time), he won the green jersey (for the points classification) and the polka-dot jersey of the King of the Mountains. No other rider has achieved this feat. He also won a record 34 stages of the Tour de France in his career.

Lance Armstrong

Eddy Merckx may have won more races in the course of his career than Lance Armstrong, but it is the American who has achieved more worldwide fame.

Armstrong was a precocious Texan who started his sporting career as a triathlete, but focused on bike racing in his early 20s. He exploded on to the world of professional cycling when he won the world championships in 1993 at the age of 21, but although he had won individual stages in the Tour de France, he was not considered a likely winner of the coveted yellow jersey.

In 1996, Armstrong was diagnosed with cancer, and given only a slim chance of staying alive, let alone recovering enough to resume his racing career. But he battled the disease, undergoing extensive chemotherapy, and made a comeback as a professional in 1998. He surprised many people by riding to fourth place in the Tour of Spain that year, and appeared at the 1999 Tour de France as an outsider. Armstrong went on to dominate the race, gaining time in both the individual time trials and in the mountain stages, and gained worldwide coverage for his comeback from cancer. He won the next six Tours after that, taking his seventh and final yellow jersey in 2005, establishing a record that will probably never be equalled, let alone beaten. In winning seven Tours, he established a new tactic, using his team to control the opposition before landing the killer blow himself.

In retirement, Armstrong continues to be an influential spokesman in the fight against cancer. He probably summed it up best himself when he said, "cancer chose the wrong guy".

Right: Lance Armstrong, an indomitable sportsman, who won the Tour de France a record-breaking seven times in consecutive years.

LEISURE RIDING

You don't have to start cycling with the aim of participating in the Tour de France. For most people, the simple practicalities of getting around town, commuting, or embarking on a short off-road leisure ride with family and friends are all that interests them. Even when cycling aims are this simple, just working on a few key skills and boosting confidence will enable you to get the most out of your cycling experience. Improving fitness will also make cycling easier and more effective.

Above: A family ride a three-seater bike through a national park in Oregon.
Left: Children ride through a field in the country.

The Hybrid Cycle

A compromise between the speed of a racing bike, and the comfort of a mountain bike, the hybrid bike is the perfect bike for the leisure cyclist who wants to get around town, but maybe strike out farther for rides in the countryside or on bike paths.

Hybrid bikes resemble mountain bikes. While mountain bikes are built to withstand punishing rides off-road, hybrids don't need to be so resilient. They have narrower wheels, and usually come with slick tyres, which offer less rolling resistance on the road. This makes them faster. Flat handlebars and an upright position mean that riding is both safe and comfortable. Some even have suspension, which makes them still more comfortable to ride.

Most hybrid bikes are also set up so that panniers can be attached to carry luggage, making them the perfect all-round bike for short and middle distance leisure riding.

Above: Hybrids are equally practical for off- and on-road cycling, and are built for comfort and speed.
Right: Hybrid bikes suit cyclists at all levels of achievement.

Anatomy of a hybrid bike

❶ Wheels: size 700x28c, which is the same as a racing bike, slightly larger than the 26in wheel standard on mountain bikes. Slick tyres for urban riding.

❷ Frame: Lighter and faster on the road than a heavy-duty mountain bike frame. Geometry is tailored for an upright position.

❸ Brakes: Calliper brakes.

❹ Chainrings: Either two or three, depending on the model. Three chainrings offer a larger range of gears, useful in hilly areas.

❺ Sprockets: There are usually eight or nine gears.

❻ Gear changers: These are mounted on the handlebars for ease of changing. Many gear changers are attached to the brake levers for good accessibility.

❼ Saddle: The saddle on a hybrid bike is wide and padded for extra comfort for the rider.

❽ Handlebars: Flat handlebars give the rider comfortable steering and an upright position.

Folding Bike

One of the most practical ways of getting around in big cities is using the folding bike.

For most city-dwellers, lack of storage space is a problem. Buses and trains often refuse to carry bikes, or restrict them to off-peak times. Once you have reached your destination, parking may be a problem.

These problems are solved by a folding bike, which are easy to carry on public transport, and can be stowed under a desk. However, they are not designed for long distance or fast cycling and they lose in comfort and speed over long distances.

Right: The Brompton has 40cm (16in) wheels, and collapses to a neat portable package.

Clothing for Leisure Cycling

For very short distances, in temperate weather, it is possible to cycle in any clothes, but if you choose practical, comfortable gear, suited to the prevailing environment, your cycling experience will be a more positive and comfortable one.

The farther you cycle, and the more extreme the weather conditions, the more you have to think about what to wear. Suitable clothes and shoes will help you enjoy your cycling, no matter what the weather conditions.

Summer wear

Staying cool is the most important consideration when cycling in hot weather. For the leisure cyclist, overheating will spoil what would otherwise be a pleasant ride. For the office-bound commuter, there is nothing worse than arriving at work covered in sweat with the prospect of sitting at a desk wearing formal work clothes.

Modern, breathable fabrics ensure that cycling clothes are light and comfortable, and importantly, wick the perspiration away from your skin. On a hot day, it is a good idea to wear a pair of Lycra cycling shorts, a lightweight undershirt and a cycling top.

A good quality pair of cycling shorts is one of the first things you should consider buying when taking up cycling. Cycling shorts have a padded, seamless insert, which makes a huge difference in comfort levels. Normal trousers are impractical for cycling – the seam will be very uncomfortable after only a few minutes' riding, and the weight of the fabric is also a problem. In the past, inserts were made of chamois leather and needed regular treatment from creams to prevent them hardening. However, modern cycling shorts come with synthetic antibacterial inserts that require no special care.

It is also possible to buy shorts or long trousers, which are not skin-tight but still have a chamois insert.

Undershirts, or base layers, are recommended to keep the sweat away from your skin. On hot days, when you are sweating, a long downhill freewheel or a breeze can cause you to catch a

chill. Over the base layer, you can wear a cycling jersey. These are also lightweight and help to keep the sweat away from your body. They also have pockets sewn into the lower back, which are ideal for carrying small objects such as keys and money.

Protect yourself

Wearing two tops while cycling will help to protect you in the event of a crash. The two shirts will slide against each other, protecting your skin to a certain extent from abrasions.

It is also a very good idea to wear cycling mitts, which have padding on the palm of the hand and cut-off fingers to prevent you from overheating. Mitts absorb sweat and so ensure that you can keep a good grip on the

Above: When cycling in summer, it is important to wear comfortable lightweight, breathable clothes.

handlebars. In the event of a crash, they will also protect your hands from painful injuries.

In more humid areas it is necessary to invest in a good raincoat. You can get special raincoats designed for cycling, which are waterproof, extremely light, and are extra-long in the back to protect your lower back from the rain when you are in a cycling position.

During spring and autumn, when the weather can be unpredictable, it might be worth considering a gilet, which is a sleeveless top, over your cycling top. This will help keep you warm in the cooler evenings.

Winter wear

The real test of your commitment to cycling comes in the winter months, when cold and wet weather can try the resolve of even professional cyclists. However, with the right mental attitude and a sensible choice of clothing, you can be as comfortable in the cold and wet as you are on a warm summer's day.

On your legs, you need to wear thermal leggings, available from bike shops. These often have bibs attached, which stretch over the shoulders to add an extra layer of insulation to your upper body without restricting your movement. These are ideal to wear in cold weather.

As in summer, a base layer is essential. Even in cold weather, your body can heat up while cycling, so it is even more important to wick the sweat away from your body. In extremely cold weather, a thermal base layer will help you keep warm. Over your base layer, a windproof long-sleeved jersey will protect you from the cold but still allow ventilation to prevent overheating. In freezing temperatures, a base layer and windproof jersey should keep you warm enough once you have started moving.

If you suffer particularly from the cold, or if the temperature has dropped below freezing, there are several ways of

Above: A thermal jacket is necessary for cycling during the winter.

adding lightweight layers for further insulation. Cycling shops sell detachable arm warmers made of Lycra, which can be rolled up or down according to what is comfortable. They are extremely compact, and when you are not wearing them they can be stowed in the back pocket of your cycling jersey.

In cold weather it is also essential to cover your head – many thermal cycling hats and headbands are designed to be worn under a helmet without compromising safety and comfort. The feet and hands need to be protected, too. Buy a pair of waterproof, thermal overshoes and thermal gloves, and you are ready to go.

Above: A warm and waterproof lightweight jacket over a base layer and long-sleeved jersey is essential when conditions turn very cold or wet.

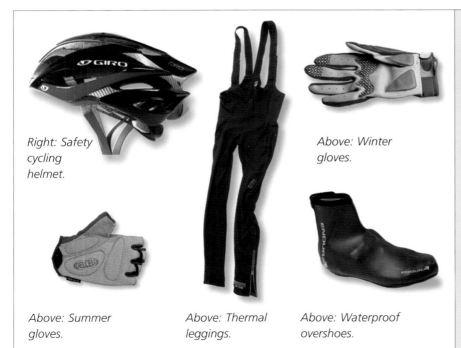

Right: Safety cycling helmet.

Above: Summer gloves.

Above: Thermal leggings.

Above: Winter gloves.

Above: Waterproof overshoes.

Cycling gear

In general, the better the shoes are for cycling, the worse they are for walking. The most efficient cycling shoes have stiff soles, with shoeplates screwed in for the pedal attachments. They make you cycle faster, but once you are off the bike, at best they make you walk like a penguin.

It is inconvenient to have to carry two pairs of shoes, one for walking, one for cycling, so a solution for the leisure cyclist and commuter is to buy cycling shoes that can also be used for walking, for example, Shimano's SPD (Shimano's Pedalling Dynamics) system. These still have plates to clip to pedals, but they are flush with the sole, which is also more flexible.

Safety is paramount, especially in the city. Wear a well-fitted helmet and high-visibility gear at all times, as well as a mask if you are concerned about pollution.

General Riding Skills

It is impossible to 'unlearn' riding a bike, and just about every adult in the Western world has a head start in cycling through learning to ride when they were a child. To regain confidence, practise on a quiet traffic-free road.

Most adults who want to take up cycling again, or even those who have kept riding throughout their lives, can benefit from refreshing their skill set. The more relaxed and assured you are about your cycling and your ability to deal with challenges and obstacles, the more enjoyable your cycling will be.

The most important thing when cycling is to feel comfortable, at ease and relaxed on your bike. Nervousness makes your body tense and affects the handling of your bike, especially the steering. On a busy road, this can prove to be very dangerous.

If you have not ridden a bike for a few years, it is a good idea to find a quiet road or a car park to rediscover the feeling of balance and flow that comes from confident bike handling. You don't have to spend weeks doing this – just ensure that you can manage the basic skills of starting, riding in a straight line, riding around a corner, and stopping. The rustiness will not take long to disappear, but it is better for this to happen away from busy roads.

Moving on

Once you are confident that you are used to riding your bike again, there are still some aspects of your cycling you should take care to work on.

Cornering should be smooth, consistent and safe. Depending on whether there is traffic around, and how tight the corner is, there are several different ways of getting around a corner efficiently.

For a shallow bend, it should be possible to just keep the line you have been following already.

For a sharper corner, take a wider approach to maintain as much speed as it is safe to have. If there are cars following behind, do not swing out into their path, but if you are certain that the road is clear, you can approach the

centre of the lane before turning as you reach the corner. What you are aiming for is to be more efficient and to go around the bend losing as little speed as possible, while remaining upright and safe.

Practising skills

Riding one-handed: *Find a quiet bit of road or a car park and practise riding one-handed, using both left and right hands. For the ambitious, it doesn't hurt to learn to ride no-handed, but don't practise this in traffic.*

Left: Practise riding one-handed to improve your balance on a bike.

Two other factors need to be taken into consideration when cornering – the weather, and the road surface. In dry conditions on a smooth road, it is natural to lean with the bike as you go round a corner, though when you do this you should keep your head level. But in wet conditions, especially if there are drain covers in the road, or on loose surfaces such as gravel, leaning the bike too far will result in the wheels sliding out from under you. There is no need to slow right down unless the corner is very sharp, but to compensate for the lack of grip, try leaning your body while keeping the bike as upright as possible. This will ensure your safety, while maintaining speed around the corner.

Looking ahead: *Once you are confident of your riding skills, get out on the road and cycle. Practise predicting what is going to happen consciously, before trying to make it a subconscious part of every ride you do.*

Drills to improve your skills

Cornering 1: *Find some quiet roads, and practise riding a loop. Plan your route through the corners and learn what your safe speed is. Push your limits, but be careful and sensible.*

Cornering 2: *Find a downhill section of road with good visibility and corners going left and right. Ride down a few times, learning to look ahead and plan your route through the corners.*

Cornering 3: *Once you have ridden around the route, try getting around the corner in a smooth and consistent way. Try not to lose speed but stay upright, relaxed and safe.*

Cornering 4: *Once you have got around the corner, maintain your speed and cycle confidently on. Always be aware of other road users such as cars and buses or heavier vehicles and be prepared to take avoiding action.*

Braking: *Find a quiet downhill bit of road. Ride at various speeds and work on getting your stopping distance down to a safe minimum. Start with the back brake to check speed and maintain control, then the front brake to stop.*

Go with the flow

Once you are cornering confidently and riding at an efficient speed, you are more in control of your bike. And the good news is that the more time you spend cycling, the more natural these processes will become.

Once you have got used to the way your bike handles, and the way you react to it, you will notice that you will stop thinking of yourself and the bike as separate entities, but don't relax too much – you still need to be ready to react to surprises.

Above: The more cycling you do, the more you will be focused.

Braking, Gearing and Riding Safely

Once you have spent some time cycling on the roads, you will become aware that the average bike ride throws up hazards, obstacles and challenges when you least expect it. Learning to anticipate these things is key to becoming a more proficient rider.

Awareness is seeing what is going to happen on the road ahead a few seconds before it actually does. By watching the behaviour of others, you can learn to predict even the seemingly unpredictable. If a car is about to turn across you, it is safer to slow down. Pedestrians may wander into the road, assuming that if they cannot hear a car, there is nothing coming. Cars can pull out directly into your path. If you anticipate, you can avoid problems. Always be aware of what is going on around you.

Braking

Reacting to an obstacle can involve one of two things – evasive action, or braking. If you have the time and space to swerve around a pothole, pedestrian or other obstacle you can maintain your speed without wasting energy.

More often, you need to check your speed or even stop suddenly, and there is a technique to this. Slamming on both brakes can cause a rear-wheel skid, or worse, a front-wheel lock, which is as potentially painful as it is embarrassing. The aim is to be in control of the bike at every moment, and controlled and assertive braking is part of this.

The correct technique for braking is to rely more on the rear brake at high speed, and then the front brake as you decelerate. As weight is transferred forward during braking, there is a

Right: When waiting at a stop light, keep one foot on the pedal, ready to accelerate away.
Below: Build the confidence to ride safely in traffic – anticipate what is ahead, be aware of what is behind.

Dos and don'ts of riding in traffic

Do Make sure that your bike is in good repair – sudden breakages can cause your bike to veer or crash.

Do Wear visible clothing, especially at night or in poor light.

Do Have working front and back lights, day or night. Overcast conditions can affect visibility.

Do Concentrate.

Do Relax, even when confronted by challenges. Tensing up can affect steering.

Do Look and plan ahead. Look out for potholes, junctions, manhole covers, cars, pedestrians, stones, animals and other cyclists.

Left: Cars should give cyclists plenty of room. When one comes past, stay focused and relaxed.

Don't Listen to music while you are cycling – you absolutely need to be aware of approaching traffic, just in case they are unaware of you.

Don't Approach junctions at full speed, unless you have full visibility and you are certain there is no traffic approaching. Check your speed until the way is clear.

Don't Assume that a driver, pedestrian or cyclist has seen you until eye contact has been established. Err on the side of caution.

Don't Ride faster than your skills and confidence allow.

Don't Ride the same in the wet as you would in the dry – stopping distances are greater. Also watch out for drain covers, which are like sheet ice in the wet.

tendency for the back wheel to skid, so try and push your own weight backward on the bike to compensate for this. It is a lot to think about for something that has to happen in a split second, but practise it until it is second nature. In most cases, the anticipation you have been developing will enable you to see hazards unfolding well in advance, and you will be able to slow down while remaining in control.

Sometimes you have to perform an emergency stop. Try never to panic and just grab at the brake levers, but stay

Left: Cyclo-cross riders keep their weight far back when braking, so that they can maintain control and traction.

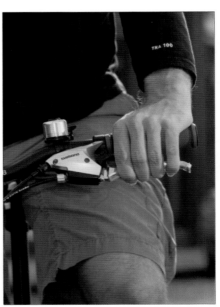

Above: Potholes can be a danger for cyclists. If possible, look ahead and avoid them, but don't swerve into the road.
Left: When braking, maintain a firm grip on the handlebars and squeeze the brake gently to control speed.

relaxed and calm and be confident that a well-maintained set of brakes and the correct techniques will enable you to stay safe.

Using gears efficiently

Cycling effectively is not about getting from A to B as fast as you possibly can. If you start a ride sprinting, you won't last long. The important thing is to ride

at an efficient speed. Choose a gear that you can comfortably turn at 60–80 revolutions per minute, just over one per second, or whatever feels comfortable. Racing cyclists prefer a faster rhythm, but for leisure riding and commuting the main aim is economy of movement.

If you are going up an unexpected steep hill, you need to get the timing right. Lighten pressure on the pedals so you can shift down a few gears. Change up if you are going downhill. On varied terrain; uphills and downhills, the aim is to keep the same cadence.

Urban Cycling

The bicycle is the perfect mode of transport in an urban environment. A bike can squeeze through a gap when the road is blocked with traffic. There are health and fitness benefits too, and cycling is a great stress reliever.

Cars get stuck in traffic jams, and once they arrive at their destination, there is scarce space for parking. Buses and trains and even underground systems are better, but you are forced to go where they go. You also have to pay for the privilege.

If the closest train station is a 10-minute walk away from your destination, you often have no option but to walk. Cabs? More flexible, but the costs quickly mount up.

Cycling offers the best of all worlds – it's free, once you have bought a bike. It's fast. You can go exactly where you want to. And it is environmentally friendly.

More and more big cities around the world are starting to realize that congestion is a major problem, both economically and practically. It is also suspected that there are major health risks involved in having to breathe the emissions from cars stuck head-to-tail on the city's streets. So, following the lead of cities like Amsterdam in Holland, bike lanes are being laid and provision for bikes is being included in many metropolitan transport plans.

Getting around

So why not go by bike? For city dwellers, most journeys are made within a small radius, well within cycling distance. If you calculated the typical journeys you make in the course of a week, along with the mode of transport you use, you might realize that many hours spent on buses or trains could be spent cycling instead. You'll save money as well as getting fitter. It's not just going to and from work that might be

Left: Panniers fit on a bike and let commuters and urban cyclists carry their gear without a destabilizing backpack.

Above: Finding a parking space for a car if you want to go for a coffee is difficult in most cities, but cycling can take you right to the door of the café.

better by bike. Weekend day trips to a museum or exhibition could be even more fun by riding there and back. If you are a member of a sports, music or social club of any description, the act of cycling could become part of the routine of your hobby.

For a night out on the town, though, the bike is not the best mode of transport unless you stick to non-alcoholic drinks.

Shopping by bike

While it is easy to imagine travelling more within cities by bike, the idea of shopping by bike still puts some people off. Getting to the shop on a bike is straightforward, especially when it is not too far away. But getting back laden down with food or fragile goods can be difficult, or even dangerous, if you're not properly equipped.

The main problem is how to transport heavy shopping on your bike without affecting your ability to ride safely. With small loads it is possible to ride with a comfortable backpack. Backpacks are not ideal for cycling – they over-insulate your back and make you sweat uncomfortably. They also affect the handling and balance of your bike. If they are not fitted correctly, it's possible for them to slide off to one side and unbalance you. If you are riding with a backpack, make sure it is secure.

Left: Cyclists can conveniently carry light shopping in a basket fixed to the handlebars of the bike.

With most hybrid and leisure bikes, there are attachments on the frame for panniers, and for heavier loads, these are ideal. A pair of bags on a rear pannier should be able to accommodate a substantial amount of shopping. You can also attach an ordinary bag to the top of the rack with bungees, but check it is secure. The weight does affect the handling of your bike, but it is easy to get used to, and once you adjust to the extra weight, it won't slow you down too much.

Once you have got used to this, it is by far the easiest way to go shopping. Your bike is taking the load for you – even when you drive to the shops, you have to carry your shopping to the car, and then again at the other end. For very large loads, it is worth considering a detachable trailer. These hook on to the back of your bike, and can be pulled along. If you are cycling to keep fit, the extra work involved in pulling a laden trailer will have a substantial effect on your fitness levels.

When you start to cycle more, the planning of journeys becomes a major part of the exercise. Plot an interesting route down roads that avoid the main traffic arteries of the city, and you will discover new areas, streets and buildings. Exploration doesn't have to take place in the wilderness to be fun.

Above: Bikes are the ideal form of urban transport – cities are too congested for most people to consider driving.
Right: A young child can be transported by bike, strapped in a seat on the back. You may not want to risk cycling in heavy traffic, though.

Commuting by Bike

If you live close to your office, there are many reasons to choose cycling as your method of transport. Door to door, cycling to work can save you time and you also do not have the expense of a bus or train ticket.

Cycling 16km (10 miles) a day will have a massive effect on your fitness level if you have been leading a sedentary lifestyle. If you cycle five times a week, there is no need to take out an expensive gym membership, which will save you time and money. Add this to the saving on travel tickets, or petrol and parking, and you will have substantially more money in your pocket. You will arrive at work fresh and invigorated from the exercise and the fresh air, even when it is raining. This will have a positive effect on your performance at work.

There is evidence suggesting that cyclists are less affected by pollution from car emissions than the drivers of the cars themselves. Cyclists' heads are above the level where the air is most polluted, while car ventilation systems take in all that polluted air and feed it straight into the vehicle. Of course, vehicle emissions are still a problem for cyclists, and you can buy lightweight face-masks that cover the mouth and nose and filter out pollutants and dust.

If you live up to 16km (10 miles) away from your office, commuting by bike is worth trying – your journey time might increase to somewhere between half an hour and an hour, but this is still less time than many people spend on public transport.

If you are starting from scratch, it is advisable not to try cycling to and from work five times a week. Suddenly going from no exercise to 160km (100 miles) in five days is a big jump. It is a good idea to plan a system whereby you ride to work one day, then get the train home. The next day you take the train in, and cycle home. You can build up from there.

If you live farther than 16km (10 miles) away, commuting by bike is still a viable option. Build up to the greater distance

Left: By riding to work you can save money on transport and gym membership – you'll get all the exercise you need.

Above: Cycling to work keeps you fit, is faster than driving and allows you to enjoy the fresh air.

slowly, and take days off if you are tired. You could consider splitting your journey by cycling part of the way and using public transport for the other part.

Arriving at the workplace
Once you have taken the decision to start commuting by bike, it helps if your office or workplace has a shower so you can wash and change before work. Many employers provide showers these days, which is the first concern of many would-be bicycle commuters. If yours has not, start to press for one to be installed. The practical benefits for the cyclist will far outweigh the initial investment in time and money. Second, you will need somewhere secure and preferably dry to store your bike during the day. Some workplaces have bike-locking facilities. If yours does not, ask

for some to be installed. If you have a folding bike, however, you can fold it quickly and store it neatly out of the way under your desk.

Lock it up

Finally, invest in a heavy-duty bike lock. The thicker and stronger your lock is, the harder it is for thieves to cut through it. Cable locks, or simple chains, will deter some attempts at theft, but a rigid D-lock is more secure. These items are bulky, but bike security is essential. Leave a lock at work if you don't want to carry it back and forth every day. For peace of mind, some cyclists even use two locks.

Make sure you lock your bike to something secure – a set of railings or a purpose-built bike stand. Some bike stands have brackets screwed to the wall – beware of thieves unscrewing the brackets and taking away your bike, heavy-duty locks and all.

All change

Now that all the facilities are in place for you to cycle to work, the key thing is to be organized. Given that arriving at work in sweaty cycling gear and then doing a day's work is probably unviable

Below: Parking problems will become a nuisance of the past when you commute by bike. Just lock up your bike at a dedicated cycle rack and go.

in most offices, you'll have to make sure that you have clothes to change into. Some bike commuters carry enough clothes for a week in on a Monday morning, then take it all home again on Friday. Others prefer to take fresh clothes in every day.

If you take fresh clothes in to work every day, experiment with the best way of folding your shirts to keep them pressed and the rest of your clothes crease-free. Carefully fold ties, or pay the consequences.

The less you have to carry, the easier your cycle ride will be. Pack a spare set of clothes, perhaps a laptop computer and diary. A good idea is to pack all your clothes and other items in plastic bags within your panniers or backpack to keep them dry in wet conditions.

On your bike

Now you are ready to go. In time perhaps you can start experimenting with different routes – a short deviation might add a mile or so to your journey, but may lead you to discovering new areas and finding a more scenic route. How many people who take the train get that opportunity?

Above: What to pack when commuting to work by bike: clothes, your laptop, bike lock, and plastic bags (top) and work papers and notebook (above).

Above: A light backpack.

Checklist
What to wear
Cycling shoes
Cycling shorts
Base layer
Cycling jersey
Helmet
Mitts
What to pack
Laptop
Diary
Papers
Underwear
Trousers/skirt and shirt
Tie
Secure bike lock
Plastic bags
What to keep at work
Shoes
Towel
Toiletries
Spare cycling kit in case of rain during ride

Mountain Biking: Getting Started

At some point, the ambitious leisure cyclist will want to broaden his or her horizons and take on the challenge of going for an off-road ride. Mountain biking is fun and user-friendly: you can ride the bike on and off the road.

Mountain biking off-road confers two immediate benefits. First, there is no traffic, save other cyclists, walkers and horse riders, and in general these three groups of people have learned to coexist harmoniously. (When riding on the trails, ride with tolerance and consideration, and everybody else should do the same.)

Second, in the unfortunate event of a crash, there is a higher likelihood of having a soft landing.

Unless you are riding on steep terrain, the same rules apply to off-road riding as to riding on the road. The specific skills of trail riding will be explored later in the book, but the main skill set is the same as for road riding, with the loose surface of most off-road paths taken into account.

Mountain biking in the countryside is one of the greatest pleasures of cycling, and it is a genuine social activity. If you are a recent convert to leisure cycling or commuting, mountain biking is a great way to get even more out of your bike.

Getting started is as easy as it is for road cycling. You need a bike and a healthy dose of enthusiasm. You can even use the same clothes and equipment, although you will need some proper mountain-biking shoes, which are good for walking, but that also clip in to your pedals.

The rough and the smooth

The biggest difference between road cycling and off-road cycling is obviously the surface on which you ride. Gravel and potholes aside, roads are uniform as well as predictable, while country paths are precisely the opposite. On a single ride, the surface can be soft mud, hard earth, gravel, rocks, grass or any combination of these surfaces. Learning to cope with the change in the surface, and the way it affects the handling of the bike, is important if you want to improve.

On most surfaces, the thick knobbly tyres on mountain bikes are capable of offering more grip than slick road tyres. On gravel, rocks or soft wet surfaces, however, cornering can still be hazardous. Approach bends with caution, and treat them as you would on a road bike, maintaining as much speed as possible, while staying within the bounds of safety.

Because of the bumpy surface on most off-road bike rides, mountain biking is more tiring. It is important to save energy by relaxing as much as possible, holding the handlebars in a firm but relaxed grip, and allowing the arms to be used as shock absorbers. If your bike has suspension forks, or is a full-suspension model, your ride will also be far more comfortable.

Braking also has to be treated with more caution, because of the tendency of wheels to lock up on loose surfaces. The front brake is the more powerful,

Above: The benefits of mountain biking are clear: it's just you, your bike and a spectacular landscape.

but use the back brake to control your speed, and the front brake to slow down more quickly.

Lastly, gearing is an important consideration. Because the hills tend to be steeper and more unpredictable, you can easily grind to a halt if you don't change down soon enough. If you see a hill coming, try to assess the steepness, and as you hit the bottom, change into a gear you know you will be able reach the top in. It's much better to err on the side of caution – if you stall, it is hard to get going again.

Above all, the best way of improving your cycling technique and to enjoy off-road riding more is to practise regularly and get used to the way your bike reacts on the different terrain.

Drills to improve your skills

Braking 1: *Find a slightly downhill section with a loose surface. Build up a little speed, then bring yourself to a fast but controlled stop using both brakes.*

Braking 2: *On a steeper downhill path, repeat. Push your weight back, start to slow down with the back brake then the front brake once deceleration is controlled.*

Reactions: *Riding on a downhill path with a loose surface and corners, keep the same speed and avoid rocks. Be sensitive to the way the bike reacts.*

Gearing: *Find a section of path that goes up and down hills in quick succession. Change gear for the uphill section as you reach the bottom, and continue with no loss of momentum.*

Balance 1: *Ride along a camber, that is, across the slope of a hill, holding out your 'uphill' leg for balance if necessary. Prevent your bike from slipping downhill as you ride along the camber.*

Balance 2: *Ride on a very loose or unpredictable surface, making quite exaggerated turns on corners to test your reactions and balance. Try this on a flat surface first.*

Choosing a Mountain Bike

With such a wide range of off-road bikes available, it can be hard to choose what type to buy, let alone a specific model. When buying a bike your needs, budget and ambitions all have to be taken into consideration.

Before taking the plunge to buy a bike, you have to decide whether you want a specific bike for a specific task, or a more versatile model to allow you to explore more than one branch of off-road cycling.

Specific bikes are easy to decide on. If you want to ride trials, only a trials bike will do – the specification is so exact and developed that a normal mountain bike will be unable to meet performance needs. You really need a downhill bike for cycling down hills properly. It is possible to ride down some courses on a hardtail bike with suspension forks, but

Right: For trials riding, you'll need a specialized bike.
Below: A full-suspension mountain bike is suitable for heavy-duty off-road riding.

you will have to keep your speed so low to cope with the bumping and shock that it will detract from the fun.

If you decide that you are going to ride off-road, then you need a more general bike, and this is where the massive choice starts to get confusing. You might be more specific, and decide that you want to race cross-country, but then you have to choose between hardtail and full suspension, V-brakes or disc brakes, even between eight- and nine-speed freewheels.

For those who just want to enjoy the occasional bit of trail riding, a hardtail bike with V-brakes and suspension forks will probably return the maximum benefit. A bike like this is versatile enough to be ridden on the trails and make it a rewarding experience, but it is

Above: A downhill bike is designed for one purpose only – it's too heavy to ride back up a steep slope.

not so specialized that it can be used only for this purpose. There is also the advantage that it can be used as a runaround urban bike and fulfil that function perfectly well.

If you are going to take the sport more seriously and hit the trails on a regular basis, perhaps embarking on longer challenge rides, your equipment needs to be a bit more specialized.

There is no easy answer to the hardtail versus full suspension debate – the topic has been debated for years. All you can do is make your own decision, based on what you think you will get out of each type of bike.

If you are light and good at climbing, you might consider going for the full suspension – the extra weight will slow you down on the hills, but as you climb fast, you can afford to slow yourself down marginally. On the other hand, when it comes to bowling down the other side of the hill, the full suspension will allow you to maximize your speed and efficiency. Likewise, an occasional

rider who prefers a bit of light trail riding on a warm day might not need to install disc brakes, when V-brakes will do just as well. If you are planning to go out in all weathers throughout the year, disc brakes are probably the right option. The most important thing is to

Above: Hardtail mountain bikes are good for off-road riding, and are more efficient for all-purpose riding.

work out which bike will give you the most enjoyment and let you cycle effectively.

The Hardtail Bike

Hardtail mountain bikes are light and fast and handle precisely, and they are excellent for speed and efficient climbing. The front suspension provides comfort and control of the bike and the fat tyres allow smooth riding on roads.

A basic mountain bike, either with suspension or regular forks and a normal aluminium frame, is known as a hardtail. Although full-suspension bikes are currently popular for their greater shock absorbency in bumpy conditions, a traditional hardtail can still be the best bike for basic cross-country and trail riding. They are lighter than full-suspension models. They also have the advantage that, combined with slick tyres, they make a far better road bike. When buying a mountain bike, it is easy

Right: Gear shifters are located on the handlebars for quick changing.

Anatomy of a hardtail bike

❶ Frame: Aluminium frame, compact, but with plenty of clearance for fat tyres. Skinny seatstays absorb much more impact.

❷ Fork: Suspension fork for shock absorption and a more comfortable ride on rough and bumpy surfaces. Most forks can be adjusted for shock absorbency, depending on the type of terrain.

❸ Wheels: 32-spoked wheels, with 26in rims, which are smaller than those on a road bike. Width can be 1.5–3in.

❹ Tyres: Thick and knobbly for extra grip on loose surfaces.

❺ Chainrings: Triple chainrings offer more possible gears.

❻ Sprockets: Eight or nine, depending on preference and model.

Much wider spread, to give very low gear options for steep hills.

❼ Brakes: V-Brakes for greater stopping capacity than regular callipers. Disc brakes are becoming more popular for their efficiency in all weathers.

❽ Gear shifters: Integrated into brake system for ease of access.

❾ Saddle: Comfortable, supportive saddle, good for rough terrain.

to be impressed by the sophisticated technology of full-suspension designs, but depending on your needs, hardtail mountain bikes are resilient and reliable. Hardtails are more sensitive to accelerations, giving a more responsive ride, which purists and traditionalists prefer. For general fitness riding and enjoying getting out on the trails, a basic hardtail model with eight-speed freewheel and V-brakes is a good choice.

Above: Disc brakes are powerful enough to check speed even on loose surfaces and down steep hills.

Frames and components

The majority of hardtail frames are aluminium, and they are compact and low. A long seatpin, small frame and 26in wheels, which are smaller than road wheels, keep the rider's weight low to the ground. This makes the bike more controllable at low speeds, either going up steep hills, or dealing with highly technical sections. Riders often have to jump off their bikes, and a low top tube makes this easier.

The triple chainset, with chainrings with 42, 32 and 22 teeth, plus an eight-speed freewheel is a good combination for riding your mountain bike over a

variety of terrains. On very steep hills, which you can often encounter on a trail ride, the inner chainring should be able to deal with the gradient.

Brakes can be either disc or the traditional V-brakes, depending on what you want to get from your riding. Disc brakes perform better in bad

Above left: Suspension forks and disc brakes help control your bike.
Above: Chunky tyres are necessary for off-road riding, to aid grip.

conditions, and overall, offer more stopping power. V-brakes are simpler and lighter.

Full-suspension Cross-country and Downhill Bikes

In recent years, the technology of full-suspension frames has improved significantly. For trail riding, the full-suspension bike gives a much more comfortable ride, which is especially important when riding long distances.

Bumps and shocks tire and bruise the body – riding a full-suspension bike can reduce these shocks and make the experience of trail riding positive and even more enjoyable.

Full-suspension bike

There is no doubt that riding a full-suspension bike down hills is easier than on a hardtail, on which all the bumps you ride over are transmitted straight to your saddle area. The suspension irons out the lumps and bumps, giving a faster, more comfortable ride.

The payoff for the extra comfort, however, is reduced speed and extra weight. Full suspension adds a few kilograms to the weight of your bike, because of the extra tubing and machinery involved in the suspension system. Every time you ride up a hill, you will be carrying more weight than a

Below: Full-suspension frames make for a less harsh ride over bumpy ground.

Above: Keep your mountain bike clean and well maintained – riding off-road in poor conditions can wear down components very quickly.

traditional hardtail, and the efforts quickly mount up and can tire you out. However, the more technical the terrain, the more the full-suspension bike comes into its own. So over the course of a long ride, including uphills, downhills and technical sections, the full suspension will probably have a net benefit effect on the speed of your ride.

Downhill mountain bike

With most other types of mountain bike, riders always have to compromise between speed and comfort. The downhill mountain bike is designed purely to absorb bumps and shocks. Downhill mountain biking has its roots right back in the origins of the sport. The first mountain bikers were the Californians who rode general-purpose bikes down Repack Hill in the 1970s, and the tradition has continued to the present day, when the downhill is a major event in the World Cup series, attracting huge crowds with spectacular races. Downhill cycling is a time trial from the top of a hill to the bottom, with bends, jumps and steep straights on which riders can reach massive speeds, sometimes over 95kph (60mph). The downhill bike, more than any other, relies on strong suspension with a great deal of travel (amount of give in a suspension system) to absorb the shocks at speed. It also needs to be manoeuvrable – courses often include sharp bermed (high-sided) corners and narrow sections that demand great control, even at speed.

Frames are full suspension, with lots of travel and large springs to absorb the impact of bumps that are hit at 80kph (50mph). The fork suspension travel is enormous, since it is the front wheel that takes the brunt of the hits. Controlling speed effectively means that disc brakes are the only real option, as they have a larger braking surface than regular mountain bike V-brakes. The chain is kept in place with a retainer, and the chainring is protected.

The riding position on a downhill bike is not over-streamlined, in spite of the fact that aerodynamics are important. The saddle is kept low, to keep the rider's weight close to the ground and the bike stable.

Above: The travel on full-suspension bikes can be altered depending on the terrain you expect to encounter.

Anatomy of a full-suspension cross-country bike

1 Full-suspension frame: Provides greater shock absorbency, and greater control and traction in rough terrain.
2 Suspension fork: Takes all the impact where the bike feels it most – at the front wheel.
3 Brakes: Disc brakes are essential for better stopping power at speed and

for cycling in poor conditions such as mud and water, bumpy surfaces and rocky roads.
4 Wheels: Rims are 26in with 32 spokes for lightness and strength. Width is 1.9 or 2.1in, for the right balance between grip and rolling resistance.

5 Tyres: Thick knobbly tyres grip the ground in rough terrain.
6 Gears: Nine-speed freewheel, combined with a triple chainring with 22, 32 and 42 teeth.
7 Pedals: Reversible clipless pedals so that the shoe can clip into either side of the pedal.

Clothing and Equipment

The varied conditions experienced when out mountain biking mean it is a sensible idea to wear specialized clothing that will minimize discomfort. Comfort is a priority as well as protection from the cold and wet.

In the summer, clothing is simple. A pair of shorts, plus a base layer for your top, and a loose cycling jersey are the most comfortable option. Some mountain bikers wear skin-tight Lycra road-racing shorts, while others prefer the look of baggy shorts, but be careful of catching them on your saddle as you stand up on the pedals. Jerseys do not need to be as tight fitting as those of road riders, since speeds are lower and aerodynamics less important. A loose-fitting jersey will help keep you cool.

Gloves are essential. No one is immune from crashing, and you will need to protect your hands and fingers if you stack your bike. Full-fingered gloves are advisable for off-roading.

Helmets, too, are just as important for off-road riding as they are on the road. If you come off, you could be seriously injured if your head hits a rock or tree roots.

If you are not planning on having to put your feet down, you can use stiffer-soled shoes similar to those of road cyclists. However, most mountain bikers will want the kind of shoe that clips into your pedals, but is also comfortable and

Above: Extreme conditions make it necessary to wrap up warm.

flexible for walking. For steep sections of trail you may need to dismount and walk, and it helps to have some grip.

In winter it is important to dress well because of the wet conditions. Depending on how mild or cold it is, you may need a windproof and waterproof jacket. Even if it is not raining, water can still spray up off your companions' wheels. Long leggings will keep your legs warm and shoe covers will protect your feet from the elements. A warmer pair of gloves and a hat are also useful. Even when the sun is not shining, it is a sensible precaution to wear goggles to protect your eyes.

Left: A lightweight waterproof jacket will protect you from the rain.
Right: Keeping feet warm is important.

Mountain bike tyres pick up mud and stones and sometimes they can be flicked up into the face of the rider behind.

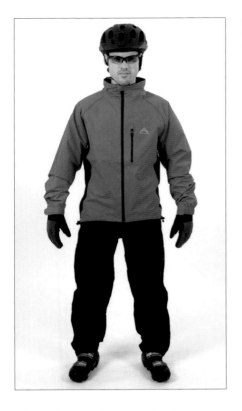

Above: Baggy winter clothing is warm and practical for off-road riding.

Above: If speed is important to you, Lycra leggings are more aerodynamic.

Above: In summer, shorts and a long-sleeved top will protect you from scratches.

Full-face helmet

Shoulder pad

Padded jacket

Shoulder pad

Elbow pad

Flexible padded gloves

Knee pads

Padded shorts

Shin pads

Downhill body armour

Downhill racers need serious protection for their bodies, in case of a crash.

On your head, you need a full-face helmet. It is not enough just to wear an ordinary hard shell helmet – these do not protect the face. A comfortable and effective full-face helmet will protect the whole of your head, as well as the back of your neck. Cover your eyes with goggles that fit inside the opening of the helmet.

Body armour will protect your arms, legs and body. Parts of your anatomy tend to hit the ground more than others and these parts have extra-hard shell protection. The knees and shins have a hard shell, as do the shoulders, elbows, wrists and chest. Downhill crashes tend to cause injuries from skidding along the ground, Full body armour, however is specifically designed to minimize this damage.

Padded downhill gloves are flexible, to allow you to control the brakes and steering without loss of sensitivity, while for your feet, protective shoes with thick soles help when you put your feet down in the corners.

Cycling for the Family

Riding a bike needn't be a solitary activity – it is one of the cheapest and most sociable ways of enjoying an outing for families and friends. In fact, if children get involved in cycling it will help them to learn a new skill and enjoy a healthy lifestyle.

Children enjoy cycling, both when they are very young and can ride as a passenger on their parents' bikes, and later, when they learn to ride themselves. The speed, freedom and fun of cycling gives children all the stimuli they need to develop, and it encourages them to explore other places.

All it takes is the attachment of a child seat, and you and your family are ready to ride. Once your children are riding their own bikes, the family ride takes on a new dimension – they can learn about independence, within the boundaries of spending time with the family.

Right: Cycling is a fun way for a child to learn independence.
Below: Going out on a ride is a cheap and enjoyable activity for a family.

Above: A flag warns that there is a child on the back of an adult's bike.

Above: A child can gain confidence by riding a bike attached to a parent's bike.

Above: Cycling is a healthy activity that families can do together.

Starting young

If you have young children who are not old enough to ride bikes, there are several ways of including them in your cycling activities. One way is to attach a child seat to your bike. Most of these fit above the back wheel, but models exist in which the chair attaches to the top tube and the child sits between your arms. Both are safe, but handling and steering are affected by the weight above the back wheel with a rear-mounted seat. The main consideration, however, is safety. First, children should always be fitted with helmets and must wear them when they are cycling.

Rear-mounted seats should have safety guards to prevent the child's feet from touching the back wheel. Another way is to get a trailer with child seats. These are designed for one or two children, and can take a great deal more weight than a bike-mounted seat. If you use one of these, visibility to other road users is very important. Attach high-visibility strips and lights to the rear, and a flag to draw attention to the presence of a trailer.

Always check the manufacturer's guidelines for the minimum age for children to be carried in their products.

For older children, who are already competent at cycling and aware of the dangers on the road, you can buy a half-wheeler, which adds an extra wheel, seat and frame to the back of your bike. Your child can even help with the pedalling!

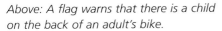

Left: Stabilizers attached to a child's bike will help him or her to achieve good balance before attempting to ride a two-wheeler bike.

Cycling for Kids

To children, the urge to explore, test their boundaries and broaden their horizons is as natural as wanting to eat or sleep. A bike is an ideal way of allowing them to do this. And once cycling is mastered, there is a satisfying sense of achievement.

It is important to give children their independence, but at the same time teach them that safety is paramount. Children should be encouraged to get around by bike, but responsible parents should explain which roads are safe to cycle on and which are too dangerous. They should be taught not to expect danger, but to be able to deal with it on

Above: Taking children on bike rides will keep them healthy and eager to explore their surroundings and the wider world.

the rare occasions it does come. The two most dangerous hazards are other road users, and children themselves. Children should be taught to be aware of approaching traffic and to avoid busy roads. Most car drivers will adjust their driving to take into account a child or indeed any person on a bike. But for the small minority who behave unpredictably, children need to be able to anticipate danger before it happens.

Once all the safety issues have been explained to children, most of the danger comes from their desire to find their limits. In doing so, they may pass their limits and crash, or fall off. In most cases, a few painful cuts and grazes are the consequences, as well as a more definite knowledge of their skill level.

For family rides together, it is best to avoid busy roads. Keep to quiet roads with good visibility, or take the children off-road and ride on designated bike paths.

For children below the age of 13 or 14, be particularly careful about planning a ride, and make sure the

Above: Get involved in teaching your child to ride a bike. Giving a helping hand can help instil confidence.

distance is manageable. A few miles at a time is enough. Plan plenty of rest stops with healthy snacks, and don't forget to take food and water.

Learning to ride

There are two ways of learning to ride a bike. The first is by experience. The second is by analysing the techniques and attempting to explain them verbally. Experience wins every time. Take your child, along with his or her new bike, to a park, preferably with grass to ride on. Explain how the brakes work, and warn them not to turn the handlebars too sharply. You can then sit back and watch as they experiment with how to keep

Above: Encourage your child to wear a helmet to protect his or her head.
Below: Once your children are proficient at cycling, take them on longer, more adventurous rides.

the bike upright. Only help if they ask for it, and be willing to hold them upright as they start, but otherwise, cycling is a skill best learned by trial and error. It will take a few goes, sometimes a few days, but eventually they will get the hang of it. Once they have mastered wobbling along in a reasonably straight line and can work the brakes well enough to stop, you can encourage

Above: Take children on rides away from roads to build their confidence and develop their skill at cycling.

them to work on more advanced techniques – turning left, turning right, speeding up and slowing down. Before long they will be fully fledged bike riders, and there will be no holding them back.

BMX for Kids

BMXs are ideal for children. They are designed for getting around without looking in the slightest bit sensible, for riding fast and for having fun on. They are perfect for riding on specially designed BMX dirt tracks, which will improve the child's bike handling ability.

Several Tour de France riders, including some of the best sprinters in the world, grew up riding BMX bikes.

BMXs are also great for stunts and tricks, either in BMX parks, which are similar to skateboarding parks, or on the street. Doing stunts is fun and safe, within certain boundaries, for kids. It is also great for learning co-ordination and balance, and building strength.

BMX tracks

It will take a while for your children to develop the appropriate skills. Encourage them to ride the BMX as much as possible without trying stunts. Once they are used to the way it handles, you can take them to a BMX track to start developing the skills to ride around it fast and safely.

Above: You can maintain a high speed riding around berms on the race track.

BMX tracks have a dirt surface and consist of a series of jumps, bumps, sloping corners or 'berms' and straights.

Good technique and balance are needed. When riding fast, the steepness of the jumps causes the bike to become airborne. Keep the BMX straight on the approach, stay straight on the jump, and land straight. Landing at an angle will cause the bike to veer and it may crash. Bumps should be ridden over, with the legs and arms bending to absorb the shock. The BMX should stay on the ground or it will lose speed.

Riders should aim for the centre of the berm for maximum speed. It's sometimes possible to pedal all the way through, but you may need to keep the outside foot at the bottom of the pedal stroke, or even to put the lower foot down, for balance.

Left: BMXs are good for developing agility, strength and balance.

Jumps and tricks

The easiest trick to perform on a BMX is a bunny-hop. These can be practised at low speed.

Stop pedalling, in a position where both your feet are at the same height, and 'crouch' over your BMX. The momentum for the bunny-hop comes from the action of the arms pulling up. Pull the arms up first, so that the front wheel comes off the ground, then pull the heels back and up (without coming off the pedals), and the back wheel will also come up. With practice, it is possible to co-ordinate these two movements so you can make them almost simultaneous.

Pulling wheelies is also fairly straightforward. As with learning to ride in the first place, trial and error is the best way to work out and maintain the correct balance.

Sitting down, pull up on the handlebars while pushing down on one pedal (this is called a power stroke). On an adult bike, the gears are generally too high to generate enough momentum, but BMX bikes have low enough gears to allow you to carry out the manoeuvre.

Extend the arms, and pull the handlebars up towards the chest. If you go too far, you can fall backwards. If you don't go far enough, the front wheel will come back down.

Bunny-hop

1: *To bunny-hop the bike, pull the arms up so that the front wheel comes up off the ground.*

2: *Pull the heels back and up. Pedal, and be prepared to jump the back wheel up.*

3: *Pull heels back and down to attempt to bring the back wheel into the air.*

4: *Land back on the ground with the handlebars straight.*

Wheelies

1: *To pull a wheelie, pull up on the handlebars and push down on one pedal.*

2: *Next, pull up the handlebars in the direction of the chest.*

3: *Keep pedalling while the bike is balanced on the back wheel.*

Improving Your Health by Cycling

Riding a bike is a healthy activity. Regular exercise in the form of cycling will make you fitter and stronger, help you reduce your fat levels and look in better shape, boost your energy and generally improve your mood.

Most everyday cycling is an aerobic activity, when muscles generate energy for movement using oxygen. Sprinting or riding up hills is anaerobic exercise, when the muscles burn energy supplies without using oxygen, because not enough is available. Aerobic activity is sustainable for long periods; anaerobic exercise is only possible for short bursts.

Unless you are training to race your bike, it is best not to get too hung up on whether you are exercising aerobically or anaerobically. Just getting out and riding will be enough to boost your fitness levels far above those of the average member of the population. You may want to push yourself sometimes, but be careful not to overreach yourself.

Effects of cycling

Cycling mainly works the legs, but the arms, back and core muscles also get a significant workout during a ride. More importantly, the cardiovascular system works hard and becomes more efficient. After just a few weeks of regular cycling, you will be less out of breath when you climb stairs, and able to sustain longer periods of activity.

Depending on how hard you go, an hour-long bike ride can burn between 300 and 800 calories. If you ride at a moderate intensity, your body will gradually burn its fat stores. If you are

Top: Regular training and riding has a beneficial effect on health and fitness.

overweight, you will lose weight cycling, but the most important thing is not necessarily to lose weight, but to reduce fat to a healthy level. Cycling burns fat, but also builds muscle, so your lean body mass may increase after a few months' cycling. This is perfectly healthy.

Incorporating the bicycle into an organized exercise routine is easy. You may wish to ride 8km (5 miles) to and from work every day, which takes no organization. Or you can set aside two evenings a week and go for an hour-long ride, plus an extra ride at the weekend. The only limiting factor is your schedule, so work with it, not against it.

Far left: Bananas are easily eaten while cycling and are a good energy source.
Left: The faster and harder you ride, the fitter you will become.

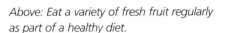

Above: Eat a variety of fresh fruit regularly as part of a healthy diet.

Cycling is great exercise, but it will have a far more positive effect on your body and health if you eat and drink properly as well. A balanced diet, with natural foods and sensible levels of hydration, will fuel your body much more effectively than TV dinners and junk food. By putting better fuel into your body you will have enough energy to continue cycling and also reap the health benefits.

If you are commuting to work, or planning on a leisure ride, it's essential to have a healthy breakfast, with cereal and fresh fruit.

If you can find a cheap source of fresh fruit, it can become extremely economical to make your own juice or smoothies. Bananas are perfect fuel for cycling. Dried fruit is good, too.

While you are cycling, it is important to eat extra food on rides longer than about an hour, to prevent an energy crash. Bananas, sandwiches, dried fruit, and cereal bars are practical. If you want to stop for a cake, go ahead – you've earned the privilege.

Eat well

After a long bike ride, replenish your body's energy supplies, or the tiredness will discourage you from going out again. There are more tasty and healthy combinations of lean meat, poultry and fish, eggs and cheese, or nuts and pulses, along with carbohydrates in the form of rice, bread or pasta, and steamed or raw vegetables than there are days in a month. Go for variety, fresh ingredients, seasonal produce and home-made sauces and dressings.

Finally, hydration is important for your general health. Cycling can dehydrate you quite badly on a hot day, so drink plenty of water. There is no correct amount of water to drink in a day – it varies enormously depending on the temperature and how much you exercise – but in hot weather, when you

Above: Use plenty of fresh vegetables and grains to make your meals varied, interesting and tasty.

Above: Nuts, pulses and cereals will provide you with energy to keep cycling.

Above: Make your own juices and smoothies from fresh fruits.

have been out for an hour-long ride, you may need at least 2 litres (3.5 pints) of water. If you are not urinating often, you are dehydrated, but there's no need to consume huge volumes of water in a day if you're not thirsty.

Getting fit

As we have discovered, cycling has beneficial effects on your fitness levels. Regular cycling makes you fit and healthy, and for many, this is enough. But why stop there? If you design a long-term training plan and work on improving steadily in the long term, your fitness will continue to improve, with all the benefits that involves. It is a good idea to build a strong foundation of fitness, then progress further by adding time on the bike, or going a little harder.

The main principle involved in gaining fitness is overload. By stressing your body's muscles the cells within the muscles break down on a microscopic level, which explains the tiredness and stiffness you feel after exercise. However, your body will rebuild those cells stronger than they were before. You will become fitter.

In turn, as time progresses and you continue to ride, you will be capable of going just a little bit harder or faster than you could before. The muscle cells will break down again, and be rebuilt stronger than before.

The fitter you get, the closer to your capacity you will get, and the rate of improvement may slow. If you are just starting out in cycling you will be amazed at how fast your body adapts to the workload you are placing on it.

Above: Use the stairs at work whenever you possibly can, to give yourself a free daily workout.

It is easy to get carried away with an exercise regime when you first start out. The training plan below will suit anyone taking up cycling for the first time, but for unfit or overweight individuals, it is best to consult a doctor before taking up physical exercise. If the most you can handle is half the time on the schedule below, then that is the correct level for you to start at.

Above: Instead of taking public transport, briskly walk – this will burn calories and raise energy levels.

In only two months it is possible to make big changes in the level of your fitness, but at this stage the most important impact on your life will be to create the long-term habit of regular cycling. If you look on a training plan as a closed period of time that is only done once, you run the risk that when it is over you will sit back, relax and let your hard work go to waste.

Stick to the programme

Follow the training plan. Swap days around if urgent appointments get in the way of the schedule. Be flexible, and keep a record of each successful ride to spur you on. After one month, assess your progression, move on to month two, and then plan month three. This way, you will have the motivation of knowing that you are fitter than you were when you started, and you have a long-term plan beyond the initial two-month period. The most important thing is to establish cycling as a regular part of your life. The fitness benefits will come hand-in-hand with that.

Left: By gradually making your training harder, your body will adapt to become fitter, stronger and more flexible.

Basic two-month training plan

Day	Weeks one to four	Weeks five to eight
Monday	Rest day but if you wish do some gentle walking	Rest day with some gentle stretches or walking
Tuesday	Ride for about 30 minutes, slow and steady	Ride for about 1 hour at a moderate pace
Wednesday	Rest day, take it easy but if you wish do some gentle stretches	Rest day but do some gentle walking
Thursday	Ride for about 45 minutes, slow and steady	Ride for 1 hour at a moderate pace; go harder up the hills
Friday	Rest day with some gentle stretches and walking	Rest day but do some gentle stretches or walking
Saturday	Ride for about 1 hour, slow and steady	Ride for 1½ hours, slow and steady
Sunday	Ride for up to 1 hour, slow and steady (optional)	Ride for 1 hour, slow and steady (optional)

Left: Make cycling part of a healthy life by riding three or four times a week.

Lifestyle choices

In our basic two-month training system, there are three or four rides a week. Just this much exercise will help you reduce fat in your body to a healthy level. The maximum amount of time you will be on your bike in a week is only 3¼ hours at the start, which still leaves more than 164 hours over the rest of the week to sleep, eat, live and work!

There are some very easy changes you can make to your daily routine to make the most of your improved fitness levels and ensure that your healthy lifestyle doesn't stop when you get off the bike.

Stretch regularly to help to loosen muscles and improve flexibility.

Walk a little faster Pick up the pace a little, so you are conscious of your body working harder.

Take the stairs Cycling builds strength in the legs – make the most of it by taking the stairs whenever possible. Yes, even if you work on the 10th floor! Walk down, too, adding to your daily exercise.

Don't use motorized transport Popping to the supermarket for some shopping? Go by bike. Attach a basket or panniers to your bike to carry the shopping.

Right: Training regularly will reduce your vulnerability to injury.

Stretches for Cyclists

Stretching helps loosen muscles and prevents the risk of sudden injury from working them too hard too quickly. To avoid injury and to gain the most from your workouts, you need to warm up and warm down properly.

Tight muscles can reduce power, co-ordination and endurance, all qualities that are necessary for cyclists.

To compensate for this, it is necessary to follow a regular routine of stretching, which will increase flexibility. Being more flexible will aid your recovery from workouts, and give you good posture and confidence to go with your increased energy levels and fitness.

With stretching, little and often is better than a long session once a week. By spending just 15 minutes after each training session stretching your muscles, you can make a big difference in your body's flexibility.

When performing the stretches on the next few pages, stretch until you feel the muscle tightening, relax your breathing, and hold the position for 15 seconds. Then release slowly. Don't bounce, or move too fast. Instead, gradually employ your muscles' full range of movement, and stay relaxed. Don't tense up any other muscles and don't hold your breath.

You should also be aware that stretching is not always a good idea. Never stretch when your muscles are 'cold', and listen to your body's reaction to stretching. If you feel sudden pain, stop the stretch and ensure that you have not injured yourself. Cyclists need to pay particular attention to the hamstrings and lower back. Tightness in one of these areas can lead to tightness or injury in the other. The hamstrings are not fully extended when cycling, and the repetitive nature of the cycling motion will eventually lead to your hamstrings becoming much less supple.

Stretch after your rides, but also after weight-training sessions, and any other exercises. For a little time and effort, you can gain flexibility, and prevent injury. Proper preparation is vital for anyone wanting to get fit. Going straight into a hard workout without warming up puts you at risk of injury and you will not be able to perform so well during your training session. If you finish your workout without warming down, your legs will be stiffer afterward and probably also the next day – if you have a workout planned for that day, it will not be as effective, because your muscles will be too tired to work properly.

A typical training session	
Minutes	**Activity**
15	Warm up on the bike
50	LSD ride including 30-minute tempo riding session
15	Warm down on the bike
10	Stretch
Total:	90 minutes

Warming up

To warm up, simply ride slowly, steadily increasing your workload until you can feel yourself breathing a bit more heavily. Once you get to this level, which should take about 5 minutes, maintain the same effort for another 10 minutes. Concentrate, focus and relax, especially if you have a difficult workout coming up. While your body warms itself up, your mind should be preparing itself for the workout. Warming up gets the metabolism fired up and ready to deal with the bigger effort that is going to follow. Your body temperature will rise, your heart will start to send more blood around your body and this will prepare your system for your training session.

Winding down

Once you have finished your workout, you need to put the same principle into reverse. Simply wind down by riding the last 15 minutes of your ride in a low gear, spinning your legs out at an easy speed. This allows your body to flush out some of the waste products that build up in your muscles during hard exercise. A short warm-down after every ride will reduce any leg stiffness you may have.

The advantage of cycling is that you can do your warming up and warming down on the bike – just build in about 15 minutes' worth of riding distance on to the front and back end of your ride, and the job is done.

Stretch after exercise

The best time to stretch is while your body is still warm after your workout. If this is impractical, stretch in the evening, after taking a warm shower or bath. Do as many of the stretches illustrated here as possible, paying particular attention to your legs and the lower back. If you feel you are especially inflexible or want to develop your stretching routine, speak to a physiotherapist, who will be able to advise you on specific exercises for parts of the body.

Above: Weight training and stretching will help to improve your performance on the bike by making you stronger and more flexible.

Head stretch

Stretches: Neck

Tilt head sideways to the left then the right then forward to stretch the back of the neck. Hold 5 seconds. Then tilt the head backward. Hold for 5 seconds.

Gluteal stretch

Stretches: Gluteus maximus

Stand on one leg, bend it slightly, then rest your other ankle on the thigh. Bend forward until you feel the stretch in the buttock of the leg you are standing on.

Lateral leg stretch

Stretches: Long adductors, inner thigh

Place the feet wide apart and lean forward so your body weight rests on your hands. Widen your stance. Rotate hips inward to stretch each leg in turn.

Quad pull-up

Stretches: Quadriceps

Stand on one leg, and bend the other leg up behind you. Grasp the foot and pull up until you can feel the quadriceps stretching. Stretch out the other arm for balance. To increase the stretch, pull the foot up higher. Repeat with the other leg.

Side lunge

Stretches: Inner thigh

Place feet wide apart, bend one knee so your weight goes down on it. Lower your bottom as far as you can toward the floor with your arms out straight and hands clasped for balance. Keep other leg straight. Repeat on other side.

Touching toes

Stretches: Hamstrings

With feet slightly apart and legs straight, raise arms above your head, stretch so the back lengthens, then bend down as far as you can toward your toes. Don't bend the knees. Hold for 15 seconds, breathing steadily, then stand upright.

TOURING

Touring on a bike is a rewarding cycling experience. Whether it is a day-trip, a weekend away, a week-long tour in a foreign country or a full-scale off-road expedition, bicycle touring is the ultimate in self-sufficient, independent and environmentally friendly tourism. Planning a trip is part of the fun, and designing an interesting route can add to the enjoyment. Keeping your baggage light is also an important part of touring. And for those with a spirit of adventure, there is the challenge and fun of camping with the bike.

Above: Travelling light is essential when touring for long distances.
Left: Touring is one of the best ways to explore the countryside.

The Touring Bike

It is technically possible to go cycle touring on any bike. The fact that you own a mountain bike or hybrid bike should not prevent you from planning short-distance tours. However, it will be better to invest in a fully equipped touring bike.

For touring, especially long distances, buying a specialized bike is a great idea. Touring bikes are light but strong: self-sufficiency is the basis of cycle touring, and the bike must be durable enough to carry a heavy load for long periods of time.

The classic touring bike resembles a racing bike, but with several subtle differences that make it ideal for the purpose. The frame has more relaxed geometry than a racing bike, which makes it more comfortable over long distances. This sacrifices a bit of speed, but bike tours are not races. The wheels are strong, with heavy-duty tyres to prevent punctures. The fewer punctures you have on a long tour, the more you can enjoy the experience of the trip.

There are fittings for panniers over the rear wheel, and often over the front wheel as well. For a long tour, it's sometimes necessary to carry a lot of equipment, and if the load is spread evenly, it is easier to carry. Many cycle tourists attach bags to the handlebars, for maps, money and anything you need easy access to, with a basic toolkit in a bag under the saddle. Mudguards are essential – they add very little to the

Above: A mountain bike is also suitable for a touring trip.
Right: Planning your route and following it is one of the enjoyable challenges of cycle touring.

weight of the bike, but keep you and your clothes drier in the case of rain (and your spare clothes will be limited).

When buying a touring bike, take time to think about which model will be best. If the longest tour you are going to do is a weekend of 50km (30 mile) rides, a hybrid bike with pannier fittings will be adequate, and good for riding around town as well.

If you are planning full-scale expeditions, covering up to 160km (100 miles) a day for a week or two, it is important to invest in a resilient, reliable and comfortable bike.

Make sure you give the bike a good test ride before you buy it, to see whether the saddle is right for you.

If your tours will include off-road riding, choose a hybrid or mountain bike, adapted and equipped so you can carry your luggage.

Above: Panniers fitted over the rear wheel can store your equipment on tour.
Top left: It's practical to keep money and maps in a handlebar bag.
Left: Allen keys, chain breaker and pump.

Anatomy of a touring bike

1 Wheels: Strong and durable, with 36 spokes to help take the weight of luggage and rider. The tyres are thick, with a good tread that will help to prevent punctures.

2 Frame: Comfortable, light and strong with relaxed geometry for riding long distances. The frame has attachments for rear panniers, pump and water bottles.

3 Brakes: Cantilever brakes for general touring. Some models have disc brakes, although maintenance is difficult with these.

4 Chainrings: A triple chainset offers low and high gears. With a heavier load, lower gears are needed to climb hills.

5 Sprockets: Nine gears at the back for all gradients.

6 Gear changers: These are attached to the brake levers to allow for good accessibility.

7 Saddle: Wide and padded for comfort during long rides.

8 Handlebars: Drop handlebars give a wide variety of hand positions, for comfort.

9 Pedals: Clipless pedals for combined walking/cycling shoes.

Touring Equipment 1

Develop the art of travelling light when touring on a bike. If you limit yourself to the bare essentials, you can go anywhere. Stick to a few guidelines and eliminate all the heavy unnecessary gear that will just weigh you down.

The number one rule in bike touring equipment is to take as little as you possibly can. That's not to say that you can leave the sleeping bag or map book at home, but superfluous equipment and items in your panniers have to be hauled everywhere – if you don't need to use something, leave it at home.

Pack a tool kit

For every trip, whether it's a day-long ride or an expedition, a toolkit is essential. You will need spare inner tubes and a patching kit in case of punctures. Allen keys for loosening and tightening bolts on the bike are useful.

A chain breaker is also necessary – breakages are rare, especially if you maintain your chain properly, but when it happens the only way to repair the chain is with a chain breaker. Perhaps more importantly, you will also need it every time you have to remove a wheel. Optional extras include a spare spoke, spoke key, screwdriver, spare cables and brake pads. It would be possible to carry a great deal more, but the compromise

Right: Always take a map on tours to keep track of where you are.
Below: If you're well equipped, you can relax and enjoy your tour.

between travelling light and covering all possible eventualities has to be made. As a self-sufficient cyclist, you are responsible for deciding how to manage the risks of mechanical failure. But never go anywhere without a chain breaker.

Cycling clothing

Sensible clothing will make touring easier. Ordinary cycling clothing is perfect – it is light, warm, and keeps the sweat away from your skin. Shoes should be combined walking and cycling shoes, with a cleat to clip into the pedals. You will need clean clothing every day for cycling, and clothes to wear in the evening when it is cooler and you are not cycling. The longer you spend away, the more you have to consider how to ensure clean clothes every day. Hardened cycle tourists work along the principle that two sets of clothing will suffice – one to wear, one to wash. This keeps weight down, but it is worth considering a small number of spare garments in case washing facilities are impossible to find.

If you are washing your cycling kit on the go, remember to bring detergent. Clean kit is essential on a long tour, because riding in dirty shorts increases the chances of a nasty and probably painful infection. Some cycle tourists wash their clothes, then they attach them securely to the outside of

Above: Bike touring is one of the best ways to see and understand other countries and cultures.

their panniers, so they don't flap into the wheel. The motion of the bike wheeling smoothly along through moving air, combined with the heat of the sun, dries and freshens their clothes in no time.

Books and other essentials

Purists would say no to carrying books – after all, they're not essential. But a little extra weight for the sake of sanity and something to do in the evening is a payoff that most people would find reasonable.

You will also need a few essential items. Buy a detailed map of the area you are visiting before you leave home. In order to save weight, rather than taking an entire map book, you can detach the pages you need and only carry them. It's also a good idea to put map pages in waterproof sleeves, to prevent damage in wet conditions. Take a wallet with credit cards, identification and spare cash. Lastly, pack a mobile phone in case of emergencies. If you are staying in hotels or hostels, that is all you will need. If you are camping, you will also need to make space in your panniers for a tent, roll mat, sleeping bag, camping stove, plate, cup and cutlery. Suddenly the third set of clothing looks like a less practical idea.

Left: Touring bikes are heavily loaded with conventional panniers at the back, as well as having capacity for extra baggage over the front wheels.

Touring Equipment 2

Modern cycling and camping gear means that you can go on a full-scale expedition without hauling several kilograms of extra weight up every hill. Over the course of an 800km (500 mile) tour, this makes a huge difference.

If you are going away for fewer than five days or if you are staying at hotels or hostels there is no need to attach front and back panniers to your touring bike. Back panniers and a handlebar bag have enough space for all the equipment you might need for a few days' cycling. If you cannot fit it all in, unpack and try again!

Panniers and tents

Front panniers become useful when you are carrying camping equipment. The main challenge is to balance all your kit equally on both sides of the bike. If your bags are heavier on one side, it will affect the handling of your bike.

A lightweight one-person tent generally weighs about the same as a sleeping bag, so a good idea is to put these on opposite sides at the back. Then cooking equipment can be split,

Below: A winding road in the Rocky Mountains, through beautiful scenery, is ideal for cycle touring.

with spare clothes going in the front panniers. Roll mats are bulky but don't weigh much – they can stay on the outside, in a waterproof bag in case of wet weather. Sometimes tents are heavier than any other piece of equipment, but it should be possible to carry tent poles on one side, and the body of the tent on the other, then various items can balance.

Try to keep heavier items at the back, while light but bulky things are fine in front. Too much weight at the front will make steering more difficult.

Things become more efficient if you are camping with a group of people. Communal equipment like tents and cooking utensils can be shared out between everybody, with individually owned items such as sleeping bags and clothes in one's own panniers.

What if it rains?

Bad weather is the last thing the cycle tourist wants to experience but it is always a possibility. Soaking wet kit will cast a real dampener on a holiday, especially if you are camping and have

Above: A fully loaded bike with a handlebar bag, panniers, tent, sleeping bag and water bottles.

no means of drying it out. Unless the weather forecast is for an immovable ridge of high pressure over the area you are camping in and bright sunshine

Below: On a cycling tour, a global positioning system (GPS) will locate your position accurately. It is ideal if you are travelling long distances.

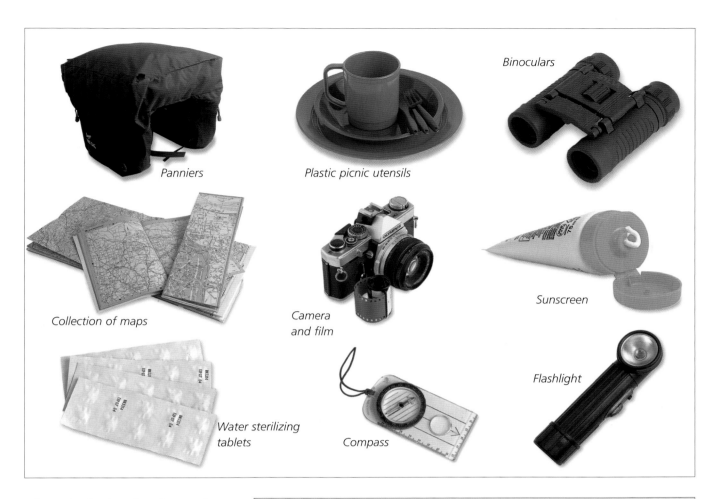

Panniers

Plastic picnic utensils

Binoculars

Collection of maps

Camera and film

Sunscreen

Water sterilizing tablets

Compass

Flashlight

Above: A selection of equipment that would be useful when touring includes panniers to fit on a bike, plastic picnic utensils, a pair of binoculars, a collection of maps to cover the area, a camera and film, a sunscreen of SPF25, water sterilizing tablets, a compass as an aid to navigation and a waterproof flashlight.

every day, it's best to bring plastic bags to put inside your panniers, to keep the contents dry. A raincoat will repel all but the heaviest rainstorms and keep your cycling clothes dry.

If all your kit is damp, and there is no prospect of a dry day's cycling, try to include an extra long stop at a friendly roadside café. While you enjoy a warming hot chocolate and cake, ask permission to hang your wet kit on a radiator or chair. The psychological boost of warming up and having dry kit to change into will make the difference between an enjoyable trip and the holiday from hell.

Touring checklist				
Equipment	**Day trip**	**Weekend away**	**Week-long tour**	**Expedition**
Rear panniers	-	Y	Y	Y
Front panniers	-	-	(Y)	Y
Cycling shoes	Y	Y	Y	Y
Cycling clothes	Y	Y(2)	Y(2)	Y(2-3)
Raincoat	(Y)	(Y)	Y	Y
Spare tubes	Y	Y	Y	Y
Allen keys	Y	Y	Y	Y
Chain breaker	Y	Y	Y	Y
Spare spoke, cables and brake blocks	-	-	-	Y
Sleeping bag	-	(Y)	(Y)	Y
Tent	-	(Y)	(Y)	Y
Roll mat	-	(Y)	(Y)	Y
Cooking equipment	-	-	(Y)	Y
Plate, cup and utensils	-	-	(Y)	Y
Map	Y	Y	Y	Y
Money	Y	Y	Y	Y
Torch	-	-	(Y)	Y
Book	-	-	Y	Y

Above: It may be useful to copy this list and tick off items as you gather them together before packing your panniers.

Planning a Tour

For some cycle tourists, half the fun of a good cycling tour is in the planning. If you take some time and effort before you leave to make sure that your bike and equipment are in good order and that you have everything you need, the tour is likely to run without hitches.

It is fun to design an itinerary using maps and guidebooks. You don't have to carve a route in stone and adhere to it religiously – you may be tired one day, or you may want to stay an extra day – but if you have a plan of your route, your tour is likely to be rewarding.

The morning of your departure is not the time to organize your cycling holiday. The first decision should be made days, weeks or even months in advance – namely, where to go. There may be a particular area whose scenery you are attracted to, or a place you want to visit for cultural reasons. You might want to go to a quiet area away

Below: Spectacular scenery is one of the many joys of cycle touring.

Above: A well maintained bike is essential: breakdowns can ruin a bike tour if you are miles from help.
Left: Before leaving for a tour of any distance, do pump up your tyres.

from the beaten track, or a region that is popular with tourists. Flat or mountainous? At home or abroad? The main thing to realize is that within limits, you are free to go cycle touring almost anywhere in the world.

Know your route

Once you have decided where you are going, you should buy a detailed road map of the area. If you are planning to stay in hotels, can you guarantee that the next town is close enough to reach in one day's cycling? You should plan your route using your map and according to your ability to cover the distance, with the emphasis on quiet roads and scenic routes. If you are capable of riding 65km (40 miles) a day, don't plan to stay in a hotel that is 95km (60 miles) from the last one. If you want to ride 160km (100 miles) every day, make sure to plan your accommodation accordingly.

If you are cycling in a mountainous area, gradients and altitudes are sometimes indicated on maps. Chevrons on the road indicate that the road is going uphill, and in high mountain ranges such as the Alps or the Rockies, hills can go on for many miles. Ensure that your gearing is low enough for you to pedal with all your equipment in tow.

Most importantly, be flexible. If you are more tired than you anticipated, stop at the next town and stay there. You are free to do whatever you want.

Preparing for the tour

Your bike should be in perfect running order before you leave. Mechanical failure could stop your tour right where it happens, so look after your bike and give it a service before your departure. After the service, take it out for a ride to test that it is running well. If you are camping, it pays to double-check that none of the tent poles have gone missing or are damaged. Erect the tent in your garden, then pack it immediately and put it into your panniers. The day before you leave, wash and dry all the clothes you are taking with you, and pack them into your bags, along with all your other equipment. You are now set for the journey of a lifetime.

Above: Touring doesn't have to follow roads – with mountain bikes it is possible to strike out across country. Many countries have trails for bikes, but it is always best to check first.

10 steps to a successful tour

1. Decide which region you are going to cycle in.
2. Plan your route, including daily distances and stopping points.
3. If you are travelling farther afield, you may need a visa. Check for any restrictions or requirements for taking your bike on to trains, ferries or aeroplanes.
4. Plan accommodation, book if necessary.
5. Clean your bike, ensure it is running well, test brakes and gears, pump up tyres.
6. Make a list of equipment to take.
7. Check that the tent has all poles and fittings. Put it up to make sure it is in good working order.
8. Wash your clothes.
9. Get new batteries for lights.
10. Pack your panniers.
Enjoy the ride!

Camping by Bike

Cycle touring is a great way to enjoy an independent holiday. When you add camping into the equation, it becomes the ultimate in self-sufficiency. There is no need to worry about finding accommodation or a suitable place to eat supper.

Modern tents are lightweight, very easy to erect and pack down to take up very little space. You can buy single-person tents that are big enough to fit one person in a sleeping bag, and they weigh less than 1 kilogram (2 pounds). Modern synthetic sleeping bags are warm and light.

Camping does make a cycle tour more challenging. A roll mat on a hard surface is not as comfortable as a hotel bed. Nor is it as warm. If it rains, your tent is waterproof, but every time you go in and out with wet clothes on, everything becomes a little damper. Sleep might not be as deep as it would be in a bed, so you will be more tired, an important consideration when you are cycling a long distance the next day.

On the plus side, you are closer to nature when camping. If you are pitching wild, rather than staying at an organized campsite, the sense of escapism is hard to equal. Away from towns that are crowded with tourists and traffic, you can discover solitude, peace and tranquillity.

It is easier to plan your route around campsites, which allow you to pitch your tent in their grounds. This costs money, but not much, and if the idea of a week without human contact intimidates you, campsites are far more sociable.

Right: When camping, stay organized and keep the campsite tidy.
Below: Camping by bike doesn't have to be a solitary pursuit.

Left: A trailer can help take the strain.

Before you even get to the campsite, you should have planned your evening meal. Many campsites serve food, but you shouldn't rely on that unless you've checked in advance. If you are looking to save money, or are not at an official campsite, you have to provide your own food. Buy it en route, so you don't have to carry it all day. This means that when you arrive at your campsite, you don't have to go on last-minute shopping trips.

Making camp

As you have practised pitching your tent before your trip, it should present no trouble once you are on the road. If you have had to split the components of your tent between panniers, remember where everything is, and have it ready so that you are not missing the tent pegs just as your tent is about to blow away.

Roll your ground mat out, put your sleeping bag into the tent, stow the panniers, and your bed is ready for the night. Usually this can be done in less than 15 minutes, leaving you plenty of time to relax. If there is more than one of you, share the work out. One person

could pitch the tent, while the other starts to prepare and cook dinner. Dinner can be heated on portable stoves available from camping shops. The most convenient ones use gas cartridges, and it is important to carry a refill for longer trips. After your meal, clean all your equipment and keep it somewhere dry. In the morning, pack your things away, and be sure to dry the inside of your

Above: Camping wild can be an enjoyable experience – but be careful to always leave sites as you found them.

tent with a dry cloth – it will have got damp from condensation and will become musty if packed away when damp. If you are camping wild, try to remove all evidence that you were ever there, especially litter.

Touring in Northern Europe

Cycling is a popular activity in the UK and northern Europe, especially in the low-lying countries of the north – Belgium and the Netherlands. The flat terrain makes it especially easy and relaxing to get around and just enjoy the scenery.

The United Kingdom is generally good for cycling tours, apart from the crowded south-east, where traffic congestion spills on to even the country roads. Luckily, outside this area, and the industrial Midlands, there are areas of quiet countryside and even wilderness. Scotland is sparsely populated and extremely hilly, even mountainous, and would be suitable for a camping

A mini tour of Devon, UK			
Day	**Route**	**Distance**	**Highlights**
Day 1	Exeter–Tavistock	48km/30 miles	Quiet roads through the wilderness of Dartmoor
Day 2	Tavistock–Barnstaple	105km/65 miles	Lydford gorge and waterfall
Day 3	Barnstaple–Minehead	80km/50 miles	Exmoor forest and moor
Day 4	Minehead–Exeter	80km/50 miles	The view from Exmoor over the Bristol channel

expedition. The farther into the Highlands you go, the more wild the terrain. North Wales is similar, with quiet roads and spectacular scenery. The Pennines, Lake District, Peak District and North Yorkshire Moors in the north of England are perfect cycling terrain. Devon and Cornwall are good cycling country, while in between all these areas are stretches of picturesque countryside waiting to be explored.

Planning a tour in the United Kingdom can spoil you for choice. Choose an area, buy a map and find the

Left: Touring cyclists pause to admire the view at Noirefontaine, Belgium.

Above: With cycle touring you can stop for a break whenever you feel like it.
Top: When you are touring on a bicycle, head for smaller, quieter roads.

extensive network of cycle paths. Most main roads also have bike lanes running parallel, which in some cases are mandatory to use, but are safe and smooth. If you are embarking on your first cycle tour, and are worried about your fitness levels, the Netherlands and Belgium are perfect – the terrain is flat, and the towns are fairly close together, so that some days you can reduce the mileage between stops. Northern Germany and France are also ideal countries for novice and intermediate cycle tourists.

Left: The unmistakable scenery of the Netherlands, one of the most cycle-friendly countries in the world.
Below: Most cities are not ideal for cycle touring, but Amsterdam should be on everyone's cycle tour itinerary.

many ancient minor roads leading between villages and towns. Take a history book, too – hidden away in unpredictable nooks and crannies you can sometimes stumble on cultural and historical treasures.

In mainland Europe, cycling is a part of everyday life, which makes cycle touring much easier. A cycling tour in northern Europe offers more in the way of cultural variety than possibly anywhere else in the world. From Belgium, it would be possible to cover four more countries – Luxembourg, France, the Netherlands and Germany – in just a few days, each with a distinctive culture and landscape. The Netherlands and Belgium, especially, are geared to cycle touring, with an

Cycling in northern Europe

Country	Terrain	Language	Climate	Notes
Belgium	Flat/hilly	Flemish/French	Warm in summer	Wind and rain common. Towns are close together – makes it easy to find accommodation.
Denmark	Flat	Danish	Warm in summer	Denmark is renowned for being expensive.
France (north)	Flat	French	Hot in summer	Beautiful cycling country.
Germany	Flat/hilly	German	Hot in summer	Hotels are expensive, but camping is cheap and popular.
Holland	Flat	Dutch	Warm in summer	Very accommodating of cyclists.
Luxembourg	Hilly	Luxembourgeois/ French/German	Warm in summer	Good camping country, and lots of very quiet minor roads.
United Kingdom	Flat/hilly	English	Warm in summer, prone to rain	Many minor roads make for good cycling.

Touring in Europe's Mountains

Mountainous regions are a challenge for the bicycle tourist, but the hard work of getting to the top of a mountain pass is usually compensated for by the sense of achievement and by the glory of the view once you get to the higher peaks.

The mountainous areas of Europe are tough terrain for cycle tourists, but offer some of the most spectacular scenery in the world.

In the French Alps, the highest mountain passes crest at almost 3,000m (10,000ft) above sea level, with climbs of up to 30km (18 miles). With a fully laden touring bike, it takes a great deal of fitness, stamina and determination to reach the top.

The Italian Dolomites and Swiss Alps are equally as hard. In Spain, desert-like conditions make for a challenging ride. There are also some very tough mountainous routes in the Apennines, in Umbria.

Training

When planning a touring trip in the mountains, preparation is even more important than on other trips. If you are new or relatively new to cycling, or are a little rusty, it is a sensible idea to undergo some training to prepare for the tough climbs. Be realistic, not optimistic, when planning your route, so that you won't spend the entire trip wishing you were anywhere else but on your bike.

In fact, training will add a new dimension to your tour and add excitement to the build-up. By acknowledging that your tour is both a bike holiday and a physical challenge, the feeling of achievement at the end of a trip will be all the more fulfilling.

Plan your pit stops

During the planning phase of your trip, look for towns along the way where you will be able to refill your water bottles and buy food.

In the mountains, towns are generally farther apart, and forward planning will ensure that you don't run out of supplies. As you are expending more energy than usual cycling up hills

A tour of the Alps, France			
Day	Route	Distance	Highlights
Day 1	Grenoble–Gap	113km/70 miles	Souloise Gorges
Day 2	Gap–Briancon	120km/75 miles	Col d'Izoard
Day 3	Briancon–St Jean de Maurienne	80km/50 miles	Col du Galibier
Day 4	St Jean–Bourg St Maurice	129km/80 miles	Col de la Madeleine
Day 5	Bourg St Maurice–Chambery	113km/70 miles	Cormet de Roselend
Day 6	Chambery–Grenoble	80km/50 miles	Chartreuse Mountains

(although the descent down the other side is a little less strenuous) regular refuelling is important. Almost every corner offers a spot with a fantastic view to rest for a few minutes and have a bite to eat and a drink.

Although the weather in southern Europe is generally warm, the conditions high in the mountains can change quickly. About every 100m (320ft) of altitude gained results in 1°C (2°F) of temperature lost. A 2,500m (8,000ft) pass can be 15°C (30°F) degrees cooler than the valley floor.

Below: Cyclists touring on the Lofoten Islands in Norway enjoy quiet roads and wonderful scenery.

While climbing, you will be working very hard and sweating a great deal. As soon as you start descending, the air is cool and it is possible to catch a chill. Stop at the top to put on an extra layer to protect you from the cool air before you begin your descent. However, you've worked hard to get to the top so enjoy the descent and remember to brake carefully into the bends.

Above: Mountain passes such as that through Wengern Alp in Switzerland are a big challenge in cycle touring.
Above left: Two cyclists ride along a road through mountains in Switzerland.

Cycling in southern Europe

Country	Terrain	Language	Climate	Notes
France	Mountainous	French	Hot in summer	Well-surfaced roads through the Alps
Italy	Mountainous/hilly	Italian	Hot in summer	Beautiful cycling country
Portugal	Hilly	Portuguese	Very hot in summer	A high level of traffic accidents – be careful
Spain	Mountainous	Spanish	Very hot in summer	Long distances between towns
Switzerland	Mountainous	French/German/Italian	Warm in summer	Not many flat areas

Above: Stop and take a break when you need to orientate yourself.
Left: When cycle touring in the Mediterranean, it can be very hot.

Touring in North America: West Coast and Midwest

Cycle touring is still in its infancy in North America, compared with Europe. On a typical day's touring in Europe, you will see tens if not hundreds of cycle tourists. However, North America has much to offer – fantastic scenery and a challenging terrain.

In North America, long distances between towns ensure that the primary means of getting around is the car. Bike touring is unusual. Why carry your equipment and luggage about on the back of a bike when you can carry far more in the trunk of a station wagon?

However, that attitude is gradually changing. Green issues are becoming more important, and Americans are becoming conscious of the low environmental impact of cycle touring.

Cycling is enjoying a boom in the States, thanks to public awareness of Lance Armstrong's seven Tour de France wins. It is now no longer a rarity to see bikes hooked on to the back of camper vans and motor homes so that when people set up camp, they can use their bikes to go and explore the surrounding area. It is only a small, logical step away from doing the whole trip on bikes.

Below: A group of cyclists on mountain bikes set off on a touring trip around Kentucky, in the United States.

Above: Big sky, big landscapes and a big adventure – touring cross country in North America.

Where to go

The west of the United States is superb cycling terrain. Whether you like hot or cold weather, arid desert or humid forest, mountains or lowlands, densely populated areas with plenty of hotels and campsites or wilderness, you will find that the western states have it all.

One of the most popular areas for cyclists, and the most rewarding and enjoyable for cycle tourism, is California, where the climate is suitable for year-round cycling.

Central Los Angeles is no place for a bike, but even just an hour out of the city, the conditions are perfect – quiet roads, stunning scenery and varied terrain. Californians need not travel to France to cycle through vineyards, when there are vineyards on their own doorstep.

Farther up the Pacific coast, Oregon and Washington both offer good opportunities for cycle tourism, although they are cold and wet during winter.

Colorado has become a cyclists' Mecca – the Rocky Mountains are very tough to cycle in – while Montana and Wyoming are extremely challenging for wilderness expeditions.

The Midwest mountain states are generally hot in summer, and the terrain is very difficult, with long distances between towns. The planning for trips around these states should

Cycling in North America

Region	Terrain	Climate	Notes
California	Hilly–mountainous	Hot	Coastal highway is a must. Go inland for hilly rides.
Canada (Rockies)	Mountainous	Cool	Wilderness, be prepared for long distances between towns.
Colorado	Mountainous–extreme	Cool	Sparsely populated, and altitude a challenge in the mountains.
Montana/Idaho	Mountainous	Cool	Long distances between towns, and challenging hills.
Oregon/Washington	Hilly	Temperate	Be prepared for wet conditions, but beautiful scenery.

take into account that it will be necessary to carry more food and plenty of water. Self-sufficiency is vitally important, as you may find yourself a long distance from the next town and source of water. You may need to camp or sleep out if it's warm enough.

Left: Many Americans take short daily excursions, rather than embarking on a full cycle tour complete with luggage.
Below left: When cycle touring in North America, you can enjoy some truly amazing scenery.
Below: Always ensure that you carry plenty of equipment and supplies on a cycle tour when there are long distances between towns.

Touring in North America: East Coast

While the West Coast and Midwest are hard touring country, the eastern half has a broader appeal. Parts of New England are remote, with tough cycling and unpredictable weather, but the East Coast and the southern states offer an easier ride.

It is impossible to generalize about such a large geographical area, but the variety of terrain around the East Coast of North America is such that the cycle tourist will be able to find something that suits his or her level. There are diverse touring experiences available, with something to appeal to everyone, ranging from deserts, plains and mountain ranges to woods. An added attraction are the roads, which are well maintained just about everywhere. There are many parks which extend for miles and which are well organized with extensive services for people who are bicycle touring. To make it perfect for the cyclist, cycle lanes abound in many states and provinces, and there are also special bicycle trails.

Bicycle touring is also made easier in North America because there are so many campgrounds that are ideal for cyclists, which are either run privately or by the government.

Flat terrain
The easiest cycling is to be found in Florida, which is very flat, with almost imperceptible undulations inland. When the highest point in the state is only 105m (345ft) above sea level, even novice cycle tourists can be confident that there will be no hills they can't manage. Although parts of the state are densely populated, it is easy to avoid the crowded areas. The weather will be the biggest challenge to a cycle tour – while winter temperatures are pleasant and temperate, the summer is scorchingly hot and prone to frequent thunderstorms.

When you plan your cycle tour holiday, always research the typical weather patterns for the time of year in which you are planning to travel.

Mountainous terrain
If you are looking for more challenging terrain, it is well worth considering planning a bicycle tour through the Appalachian Mountains. The mountains

Above: Some of the roads on the east coast are empty, which is ideal for touring. Below: When cycling in a hot area, particularly in summer, you'll need to take plenty of water.

run for more than 1,600km (1,000 miles) from Alabama, which is in the southern United States, all the way to Newfoundland in Canada.

The Appalachians are a middle-mountain range – the roads are approximately half the altitude of a typical Alpine or Rocky Mountain pass.

The Blue Ridge Mountains in Virginia are ideal cycling country for the cycle tourist who has ambitions for a challenging tour, but who does not want to endure the extreme physical exertion of a route through a high mountain range. The roads in Virginia are quiet and rolling, with forests to shelter you from the midday sun. In high summer, Virginia is humid, but apart from this time, and winter, the weather is perfect for cycle tourism.

Above: Touring through New England is a great experience; it is fantastic cycling country and the scenery in the fall is particularly breathtaking.

New England

A popular destination for cycle tourists in the United States is New England – the quiet backroads, moderate terrain, attractive scenery, temperate climate and the friendliness of the people make for good cycling country. You can choose between forested areas, farmland and New England villages. Summer and the famous New England Fall, when the foliage is at its resplendent best, are good times of year to explore.

Where to go?

With such a wide choice of destinations in North America, it can be difficult to make a decision – you may feel you want to go everywhere! The best starting point is to look at yourself and your touring companions. Ask yourself what you want to experience, and assess your ability to cover long distances or hard terrain. Factor in whether you want to ride through woods, towns or farming country, and if mountainous or flat terrain is preferred. This approach may seem coldly scientific, but your tour is much more likely to be a fun, rewarding experience.

Right: This tranquil road, which is perfect for cycle touring, goes through beautiful pastures in the Great Smoky Mountains National Park in Tennessee.

Cycling in North America			
Region	**Terrain**	**Climate**	**Notes**
New England	Hilly–challenging	Temperate	Very enjoyable cycling with a range of difficulties
Southern States	Flat–hilly	Hot	More densely populated and be prepared for hot temperatures
Virginia	Hilly	Temperate	Perfect cycling country, in Blue Ridge Mountains

Touring Farther Afield

Africa, Asia and South America are a good challenge for the more experienced cyclist. They present more difficulties than Europe and North America, but, with a little foresight and packing the appropriate equipment, the result can be a holiday to remember.

A great deal of the enjoyment and challenge of cycle touring comes from the self-sufficiency involved in completing a tour. Whether you have ridden for two short days between hotels or three weeks in the Alps, the sense of achievement comes from having relied on your own horsepower to get from the start to the finish.

For an even more challenging cycle-touring experience, Africa, Asia and South America are as tough as it gets. The climate is hotter, the roads are less well maintained and the distances between towns are potentially huge.

Right: Cycle touring can be your passport to scenery like this.
Below: Conditions can be challenging when touring in remote areas – be prepared and plan carefully.

Above: Should you have a puncture en route, carrying a spare tyre is essential.

Above: A GPS phone is useful to help with navigation.

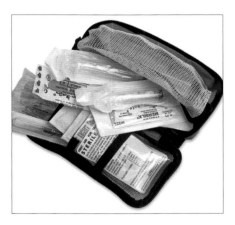

Above: Always take first aid supplies when touring off the beaten track.

You don't just have to be self-sufficient in terms of covering the distance, you have to take into account that you may need to carry more food and equipment. If your maps are inaccurate, you may even have to navigate yourself in order to get to your destination.

Remote areas

It is important to plan for every eventuality when organizing a cycling expedition to Africa, Asia or South America, from picking your destination, through making contingencies for mechanical failure, to researching the geography, roads and local people. Parts of south-east Asia have extremely busy roads, with the occasional erratic driver, but escape from the built-up areas and you will experience friendly hospitality from the people you meet.

A cycling tour in northern India should take into account the monsoon season, and the extreme terrain of the Himalayas. Avoid cycle touring during the monsoon – touring in pouring rain and extremely high humidity is no fun.

Touring in the Himalayas, or Andes, is a different proposition from the Alps. The roads suffer from weather damage in the freezing winter, and from land-slides, so surfaces are unpredictable and difficult to ride on. The altitude is higher than the Alps, with the highest road pass in the Himalayas, the Karakoram Highway, tops out at almost 5km (3 miles) – the thinner air makes exertion extremely tough. The roads can climb for around 50km (31 miles), so good

physical fitness is essential. In the southern half of India, the heat is not ideal for touring, but the terrain is less mountainous. In any country, assumptions about the weather can make or break your cycling holiday – find out the typical rainfall, humidity and temperature of the month you are visiting.

Cycle touring in China is also varied. Avoid industrial areas and the arid west – there's plenty to see elsewhere. Beijing is less cycle-friendly than it used to be, but once you are out of the city, avoid the expressways and keep to old minor roads.

Africa, on the other hand, offers wild, hot and challenging terrain. The roads range from good to non-existent. And South America is a continent of contrasts

for cycle tourists. The Andes are extremely challenging, while the wide open spaces of Brazil and Argentina make a more leisurely tour possible.

One more note – touring in Australia is fairly straightforward when keeping to the more densely populated coastal areas. But crossing the centre needs careful planning. Water stops are few and far between, and the weather is extremely hot. Self sufficiency is the key to all cycle touring, but especially in conditions like these.

Be prepared

Self-sufficiency is important for both you and your bike when cycle touring off the beaten track. If there is a problem, you cannot ride to a town and buy a replacement part. You have to carry a few more tools and replacement parts to deal with any mechanical failure. If there are long distances between towns or stops, carry your own food and water, plus water purification tablets in case you have to use a local source.

Respect local culture

In some regions, the locals are not used to seeing western tourists, let alone a group of them on bikes. In most parts of the world, hospitality to strangers is a common trait, and you can find yourself being treated like a celebrity for the duration of your stay. However, it is important to respect local traditions. If local people have their legs and arms covered, cycle tourists should be aware of the impact of cycling into town in shorts and a teeshirt. It is rare, but the locals may take exception to westerners, in their eyes, dressing immodestly or behaving disrespectfully. Common sense is the best way to decide how to behave. A friendly and generous manner will get you a long way with most of the world's people.

Extra equipment for touring

As well as all the general equipment you will need for touring, planning for certain eventualities involves carrying more equipment. It is worth taking the following items, the extra weight will be well worth it: GPS phone, first-aid kit, water purification tablets, freewheel remover, lubricants, spare tyres, various dried foods and/or canned foods.

BIKE TECHNOLOGY

Maintaining a well-running bike is part of the enjoyment of cycling. It is easy to forget to look after your bike – they are so well-designed and engineered that it is possible to run them for long periods without maintenance or even cleaning. However, failing to look after your machine could lead to breakages, inefficient running and possibly even crashes. If you do a few small jobs regularly – some every time you ride, some on a weekly basis, and some once a month – your bike will continue to run as well as it did when it was new.

Above: Set aside an area in which to work on cleaning and repairs.
Left: To ensure its smooth running, learn how to maintain your bike.

Frames and Forks

The frame and forks are the heart of your bike. The material they are made out of, the angles of their design and the quality of the joins have more of an effect on the way your bike rides than any other component.

Bicycle frames need to be light and strong. The lighter the frame, the easier it is to ride up hills. The stronger the frame, the more reliable it will be. Both these factors depend on the material used and the thickness of the tubes. There is a third attribute, which affects how efficiently power is transferred from your legs into forward motion: stiffness. A stiff frame will respond better to accelerating forces, because less power is lost in the tubes flexing, but it can sometimes mean an uncomfortable ride over long distances – there is no shock absorbency, and the rider feels every bump and rut.

The geometry of the frame also affects the way the bike handles. The relaxed geometry of a touring frame makes for a comfortable ride, but acceleration is more sluggish. A steep-angled racing frame is much faster and more responsive, but over long distances is not as comfortable.

Above: Modern bike frames are available in all shapes and sizes. This one is a lightweight mountain bike with full suspension for shock absorbency.

Above right: Wipe your frame clean every few days to prevent dirt building up.
Above left: It's important to inspect your frame and forks regularly to check for damage and denting.

Frame care		
Task	**Frequency**	**Time taken**
Wipe frame clean	Every 3 days	2 minutes
Check frame and fork for damage	After a crash	3–5 minutes

Above: A full-suspension mountain bike frame.

Above: A mountain bike frame with the suspension at the rear.

Above: A carbon fibre racing frame, which is stiffer than frames made from other materials.

Above: A steel racing frame, which is more comfortable than carbon fibre.

Looking after the frame and fork

Unlike many parts of your bicycle, which can be stripped down into their constituent elements, the frame and the fork require very little in the way of maintenance. It is impossible to take the frame apart and put it back together again.

It is important to keep your frame clean because dirt and grit can quickly build up where the tubes join, and this can lead to scratches on the paintwork. After every ride in the wet, or every few days if the weather is dry, wipe your frame and forks with a damp cloth. This takes about two minutes and is well worth the time.

Another important task is to inspect your frame and fork regularly, especially if you have had a crash. Small dents and misalignments can eventually result in structural failure.

Materials

Frame materials have come a long way since the 1980s. Steel was the most popular and the best material for bike frames for most of the 20th century. Then, in the 1980s and 1990s, bike manufacturers started using carbon fibre, aluminium, titanium and even magnesium to make frames.

Steel is strong and easy to work with. Frames made of steel are very durable – if you avoid damaging them in crashes, they can last for a lifetime.

Aluminium is a more popular choice for racing bikes and serious tourers – it flexes less than steel, weighs far less and is cheap and easy to work with but it is not as durable. Aluminium frames seem to have a 'sell-by' date after which they wear faster than steel frames.

Carbon fibre is a popular material for high-end racing frames. It is as strong as steel and aluminium, and weighs even less than aluminium. Carbon fibre is moulded into shape, so that unusual frame designs such as monocoque time-trialling bikes can be made.

Titanium is strong and light, but is expensive and therefore a less common material for bike frames.

Suspension

For mountain bikes, it is not just the materials used for the frame and fork that have changed over the years. The development of suspension has radically altered the design of mountain bike frames and the way they handle. A suspension frame will be significantly more comfortable to ride on bumpy surfaces, but the suspension absorbs energy from the rider, resulting in a slower ride. There is also a payoff in having to maintain extra moving parts.

Wheels

Your bike is not going to get very far without these vital pieces of equipment. As with frames, the lighter and stronger the wheels are on your bike, the faster you will go. A little bit of maintenance of the wheels will give you a smoother ride.

Most wheels are designed along an arrangement of spokes radiating outward from the hub to the rim. The spokes are kept in tension, which makes the structure extraordinarily strong for its weight. Some specialized bikes for time trialling use solid carbon fibre bodies for superior aerodynamics, but the basic design of bike wheels has remained remarkably constant.

The two attributes of wheels that will affect the speed of your cycling the most are aerodynamics and weight. Even on a thin racing wheel there is a significant slowing effect from the spokes passing through the air. Manufacturers try to get around this by making the rims deeper.

Bike wheels are not particularly heavy compared with other parts of your bike, but the rotational movement increases their 'weight' through a phenomenon called gyroscopic inertia, whereby the momentum of the wheel resists changes to its orientation. In short, the less material there is in the wheel, the less energy it takes to brake and accelerate.

Racing-bike wheels are narrow and light, often containing 32, 28 or even 24

spokes – weight saved by cutting the number of spokes is significant, but the compromise is in the strength of the unit. Touring bikes, which carry much heavier loads, have 36- or 40-spoke wheels. Mountain bike wheels have a slightly smaller diameter, and they range between 28 and 36 spokes.

Spokes can be arranged in different patterns, which maintain lateral stiffness.

Above: Hybrid bikes need stronger wheels – they have an increased number of spokes, which add strength.

Looking after your wheels
Wheels are your bike's point of contact with the road and they consequently take a great deal of abuse, especially from rough road surfaces. Potholes, ruts and bumps in the road can put your

Above: Narrow-section racing wheel.

Above: Carbon fibre racing wheel.

Above: Solid wheel for time trialling.

Above: Check your wheels for alignment by spinning them and watching the rim – if it moves, you may need to straighten your wheels.
Top middle: Prevent dirt building up on the hubs by wiping them every few days.
Top right: Apply grease to the axles on a regular basis.
Right: Wipe spokes down regularly.

wheels out of alignment, which affects your speed and leads to uneven braking. Learning to make wheels straight again is one of the great arts of bike maintenance. It involves mounting the

Wheel maintenance		
Task	**Frequency**	**Time taken**
Clean rims, hubs and spokes	Once a week	5 minutes
Check alignment	Once a week	30 seconds
Take axles out to clean and lubricate	Once a month	3 minutes
True your wheels (if you know how)	When misaligned	30 minutes+

wheel on a jig and tightening or loosening the spokes with a spoke key – called 'trueing' the wheel. When all of the spokes are at the correct tension, the wheel will be true, or straight, again.

Tyres

The fatter your tyres, the more comfortable the ride. The thicker your tyres, the less likely you are to suffer from punctures. But these benefits come at the cost of speed.

When choosing tyres for your bike, you must decide which kind of tyres best suit your needs. A racing bike needs slick, narrow tyres, although

Left: Thick tyres with a deep tread are used on mountain bikes.

punctures are more frequent. A touring bike needs slick tyres too, but wider, to fit wheels designed to take heavier weights. Mountain bikes need knobbly, thick tyres. These are good for puncture resistance, but much slower on a smooth surface.

Tyres are designated by size. Racing and touring tyres come in sizes between 700 x 20C and 700 x 28C (where 700 is the diameter of the tyre in millimetres and the second figure the width of the tyre in millimetres). But mountain bike wheels are generally 26in in diameter. Tyres are designated 26 x 1.5 (26in diameter x 1.5in wide) and upwards.

Always make sure you are buying the right size of tyre for your wheels, and choosing the right tyre for your needs.

Drivetrain and Gears

The first bicycles had a single gear – good for riding on the flat but hard going up hills. Gears can make all the difference to whether your bike ride is easy or difficult. Understanding your gearing system will help you improve your cycling efficiency.

Racing bikes from the early 20th century managed to add a gear by putting one sprocket on either side of their back wheel – one for uphill sections, the other for flat roads. To change gear, the riders would dismount, unbolt their back wheels and turn them around.

Then Tullio Campagnolo, an Italian racing cyclist, came up with the idea of the derailleur gear, where the chain runs through a movable device and can change on to different sprockets while the bike is in motion. This is the gearing system used on most leisure bikes today.

The early derailleur gearing system had two or three sprockets on the back wheel. As technology evolved, it became possible to have two, then three chainwheels at the front, and in the case of modern bikes, 10 sprockets at the back, giving 30 possible gear ratios.

Gear ratios are what make it possible for you to ride your bike efficiently.

In a big gear, one revolution of the pedals causes more revolutions of the wheel, but it is correspondingly harder to push the pedals around. Smaller gears make it easier to ride up hills.

The more teeth on the chainwheel (at the front), and the smaller the sprocket (at the back), the bigger the

gear. On a typical racing bike, the front chainwheels have 42 and 52 teeth, although depending on the terrain, many riders change these for slightly smaller or larger numbers of teeth. At the back, sprockets range from 11 teeth (a high gear used only on steep downhills and in sprints) to 23 or 25 teeth, enough to get up long, steep hills. When selecting a gear, keep the chain as

Above: The drivetrain consists of chainrings, which are attached to the pedals and cranks at the front, and a range of sprockets at the back.

straight as possible. Riding in the big chainwheel, which is on the right-hand side, with the largest sprocket, which is on the left-hand side, puts the chain at an angle, which will quickly wear out both chain and cogs. On a 30-gear bike, there is enough crossover between gear ratios that you can change to the middle chainwheel and a smaller sprocket to find a similar gear.

Try to avoid overgearing – professional racing cyclists can cruise along in a 52-tooth chainwheel and 14-tooth sprocket, but trying to push big gears puts a strain on the knees. Aim instead to spin the pedals faster.

Looking after your drivetrain
The chain, chainwheels, sprockets and front and back gear changers are the parts of your bike that are most prone to dirt accumulation.

Hub gears
Shopping and town bikes sometimes come with three- or five-speed hub gears, where the changing mechanism lies in a sealed unit within the back hub. These do not offer as many different gear ratios as racing or leisure bikes and they are not as power efficient. If you are too busy to maintain your bike regularly, and only want your bike for riding around town, it is worth considering buying a bike with hub gears.

Left: Hub gears require just a squirt of lubricant every few weeks.

Above: The rear mech shifts the chain from side to side along the sprockets on the back wheel.

Keeping a smooth-running and clean drivetrain is crucial for the efficient performance of your bike. If you do not clean your gearing system, dirt and grit sticks to the lubricant and forms a thick, sticky black coating that wears down moving parts, makes changing gear inefficient and generally gets everywhere. Once this has built up, it takes a lot of time and effort to clean it off. It is far better to spend 15 minutes once or twice a week to clean and lubricate your gears than to leave it for a month, then have to spend an hour up to your elbows in dirty grease while

risking damage to your drivetrain. To clean the chain, you can use a chain-breaking tool to take it off the bike. An easier way is to attach a chain-cleaning bath to the bike. These are made of plastic and contain brushes and a reservoir of cleaner. Bike shops sell degreasers and solvents that will loosen the dirt on your chain.

To clean sprockets and chainwheels remove them from the bike and scrub out the dirt with a hard brush and cleaner. When cleaning sprockets that are still on the back wheel, be careful not to let grease drip on to the rims. You can buy a brush called a cassette scraper to clean between the sprockets. Finally, the derailleurs also need careful cleaning and attention. You can

Above: The front gear mechanism shifts the chain from one chainring to another.

generally wipe a front derailleur clean, but most dirt build-up occurs in the rear derailleur. Remove it from the bike and clean all the moving parts, paying special attention to the jockey wheels.

Once everything is clean, use a light lubricant. Too much lubricant will result in more dirt build-up.

Cleaning little and often, with a major stripping-down every month or two, will keep your bike in perfect, efficient working order.

Below: Modern racing bikes have their gear changers built into the brake levers.

Drivetrain care		
Task	**Frequency**	**Time taken**
Clean chain using a chain bath	Once a week (more in wet conditions or winter)	5 minutes
Clean sprockets	Once a week	15 minutes
Clean rear derailleur	Once a week	15 minutes
Clean front derailleur	Once a week	5 minutes
Take entire drivetrain apart for deep cleaning and lubricating	Once a month	30 minutes
Clean hub gear	Once a month	10 seconds

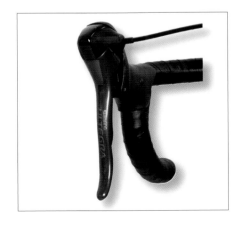

Brakes

A well-maintained set of brakes is one of the most important components of your bike. While an inefficient drivetrain or slightly untrue wheel will affect your speed and make cycling hard work, a badly worn set of brakes is potentially a killer.

Until the advent of mountain bikes, most bikes came with simple calliper brakes. By pulling a cable attached to the brakes, the brake blocks came into contact with the rim of the wheel, and the friction slowed the bike down. With narrow rims and lightweight wheels, not much surface area is needed on the brake blocks, meaning stopping performance with calliper brakes is generally very good.

Calliper brakes come in a variety of designs. Dual-pivot brakes are common on racing bikes and leisure bikes, and consist of two arms, one of which pivots around a point above the wheel, while the other pivots at the side. The arms grip the rim. They are light and useful for around-town use and longer rides, but should not be used on mountain bikes, where greater stopping power is needed, and the thick tyres get in the way.

Above: Racing bikes are fitted with dual-pivot calliper brakes, which are lightweight and provide good stopping power.

Cantilever brakes have each arm attached to a pivot point on the forks or seat stays. These have greater clearance than side-pull brakes, so they can be used on mountain bikes for riding around town, or light-duty off-roading. These brakes have generally been replaced for urban use by V-brakes, which have the cable housing on one arm, and the cable wire on the other. The longer arms of cantilever brakes provide more stopping power than V-brakes: they are also easier to maintain.

For serious mountain biking, especially on steep hills, traditional cable brakes are not strong enough to control speed effectively. Mountain bikes have heavier, wider wheels, and disc brakes, similar to those used in motorbikes and cars, can be used for greater stopping power. Disc brakes are heavier than traditional calliper brakes, but they work far better, and are easy to look after.

Above: Cantilever brakes are a good option for mountain bikes if disc brakes are not practical.
Above left: Modern mountain bikes are fitted with disc brakes, which provide good stopping power in poor conditions.
Left: V-brakes are fitted to hybrid bikes, and mountain bikes for urban use.

Brake maintenance

Alignment: *Check brakes for alignment regularly.*

Cables: *Maintain stopping power by keeping cables tight.*

Blocks: *Replace worn brake blocks.*

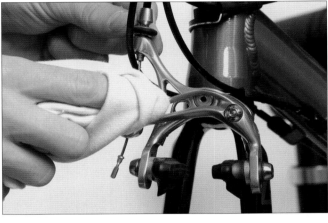

Clean: *Keep your brakes clean and oil-free by wiping often.*

There is a metal disc attached to the hub, and brake pads squeeze the disc to slow the bike down. The benefit of disc brakes is that they work as well in wet as in dry conditions. Disc brakes are used for touring, when heavier loads make stopping difficult.

Brakes wear out fast, especially calliper brakes in poor conditions, and it is important to keep an eye on the rate of wear of the rubber brake blocks. When you notice blocks getting worn, replace them – unscrew the old ones from the brake arms and put the new ones on. Never replace just one brake block, and be careful to align it with the rim, so that the whole surface of the block is in contact with the rim when the brake lever is pulled. Brake levers are low maintenance, and do not need

to be stripped and cleaned often. You should also check your cables. Brake cables stretch, with a marked effect on performance. When you notice braking is less efficient than before, loosen the cable where it passes through the brake arms, then pull it through so it is tight again. The brake arms are exposed to all the dirt and grit that flies up off the

wheel, so keep them clean. Don't clean your disc brakes too often, as tiny bits of brake pad embedded in the disc surface improve performance, but it is important to keep the disc and callipers aligned – just loosen the callipers, line them up, and tighten again. Do not allow oil to get on to the surface of disc brakes – this will affect their performance.

Brake care		
Task	**Frequency**	**Time taken**
Check brake blocks	Once a week	30 seconds
Replace brake blocks	When they are worn	5 minutes
Tighten brake cables on calliper brakes	Once a week	5 minutes
Clean calliper brake arms	Once a week	1 minute
Check alignment of disc brakes	After every ride	30 seconds
Realign disc brakes	When they are out of true	5 minutes

Bike Maintenance

You have a choice when it comes to looking after your bike. You can invest small, convenient amounts of time on a regular basis, or you can pay for inaction with large amounts of time every few months, by which time your bike is dirty, worn and inefficient.

Although you do not need to clean your bike after every ride, it will save you trouble in the long term if you clean it after riding off-road, in muddy conditions or in rain. If you leave mud or grit on your bike, the parts are liable to rust or wear more quickly. In the winter, salt from roads can affect the smooth working of the bike and lead to rust.

Keeping your bike clean

The tools you will need are a bucket of warm water with detergent, a cloth and a brush. As a general rule, try to clean your bike once a week, and less in the summer months. To hold the bike firmly, attach it to a stand. Using a brush or a cloth, wash the frame, forks, wheels, including the spokes, hub and rims, the cranks, seatpin, handlebars and stem (where they are not covered by handlebar tape), brake levers, brakes and cable housings. Rinse the parts with clean water then polish with a clean dry cloth.

Replacing handlebar tape

If your handlebar tape becomes very worn and dirty from use, or if you scuff it in a crash, it is time to replace it. This is a fairly easy task, requiring only some sharp scissors or a knife and a roll of new handlebar tape.

Take the bar end plugs off; you may need to use a screwdriver or other tool to loosen them. Fold the edges of your brake lever hoods forward so they are out of the way and expose the old bar tape. Unwrap the old bar tape, cutting off pieces here and there and discarding them. Remove any leftover glue.

Replacement bar tape usually comes with two short lengths of tape – these are for covering the brake lever clamps. Stick these two lengths on first. Then start winding tape from the bottom of the handlebars, making sure that there is enough tape at the start to tuck into the handlebar ends.

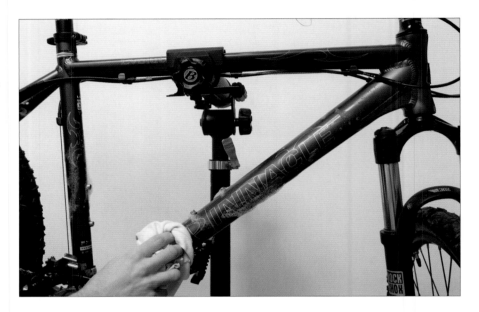

Above: Use a soft, clean cloth and detergent to wipe your frame, paying particular attention to corners where dirt can accumulate.

Keep winding round, overlapping up to half the width of the tape each time round. Pull on the tape as you are wrapping, to maintain the tension and avoid slackness, which will quickly come unstuck as you are riding.

When you get to the brake levers, work around them, making sure not to leave any part of the bars uncovered, then continue to wrap the tape around and around all the way to the tops of the handlebars.

Cut off any excess tape, and use black electrical tape to secure the end of the tape at the centre of your handlebars and tuck the other ends into the hollow end of the handlebars. Replace the bar end plugs, ensuring that the end of tape is tucked inside, and you are ready to go.

It's important to make sure the bar end plugs are firmly pushed in. Riding without these can be dangerous if you crash, and hit the bars with your leg.

Above: Brush off any grit or mud before rubbing the frame with a damp cloth, then polishing with a clean cloth.

Above: When the handlebar tape becomes worn and uncomfortable to hold, it can be easily replaced.

Replacing a tyre and tube

Tube: *Keep spare inner tubes in case you have a puncture that you cannot repair.*

1: *To remove tyre, insert a tyre lever. Keep it wedged there and insert the next. Then, lever along the rim to get the rest out.*

2: *Once you have got one side of the tyre away from the rim, use your fingers to remove it completely.*

3: *Put one side of the new tyre inside the rim, then be ready to insert inner tube.*

4: *Put the valve through the hole in the rim, put the inner tube inside the tyre.*

5: *Continue working the inner tube inside the tyre, around the wheel.*

6: *Press the other side of the tyre inside rim. Take care not to puncture the tube.*

7: *When the tube is inside the tyre and the tyre is inside the rim, pump it up.*

Basic maintenance equipment
Surgical latex gloves
Full set of Allen keys
Pliers and adjustable spanner (wrench)
Tyre levers
Track pump (upright with pressure gauge)
Screwdrivers and chain breaker
Degreaser
Chain lubricant
Freewheel remover with chain whip
Spanners (wrenches)
Bike stand
Cable cutter
Repair kit

Preventing Problems

Bike maintenance can be broken down into a few basic tasks, which, if done on a regular basis, will keep your bike running smoothly. Rather than waiting for problems to develop, it is a good idea to pre-empt these by regular, careful maintenance.

Sticking to a few golden rules will help you to keep your bike in good order. Just by getting into the habit of regularly cleaning your bike, you will familiarize yourself with all its parts and will be alert for anything that is out of order.

Drivetrain maintenance

The drivetrain (chainwheels, chain and sprockets) is the part of your bike that is most vulnerable to dirt build-up and damage. Over time, dirt from the road or bike path will stick to the chain lubricant to form a thick black coating. If this is not cleaned off, the moving parts can be damaged by the grit being ground in. Every week, if you ride your bike regularly, it's a good idea to use a chain bath to clean the chain. This is an

Disassembly, cleaning and maintenance

1 Break the chain using a chain breaker. These push a rivet through so that the links can be pulled apart (never push a rivet all the way through, as you will not be able to get it back in). Some chains, called powerlink chains, have a single link that can be unhooked manually.

2 Take the back wheel off. Using a chain whip and freewheel remover, take the sprockets off the back wheel.

3 Undo your chainrings with Allen keys.

4 Scrub all sprockets, chain rings and chain using a degreaser. If very dirty, leave them to sit in a tub of degreaser.

5 Loosen cables and remove front and rear mechanism. Scrub with detergent. Use

degreaser for a large build-up of dirt.

6 Replace cables if they are stretched by running them through from the handlebars down to the mechs.

7 Reattach front and rear mech. Pull cables through so they are taut. Tighten.

8 Put freewheel back on wheel. Replace wheel. Run chain through front and rear mechs, and reattach chain using chain tool.

9 Use a rag to apply a light but even layer of lubricant to the chain.

10 Double-check that indexing of gears is accurate (such that a single gear change moves the chain one sprocket). Adjust using the barrel adjuster on the rear mechanism.

Cleaning bike parts

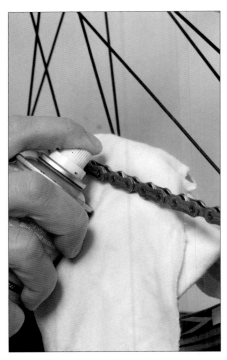

Chainwheel: *Use warm water with detergent to clean your chainwheels regularly and prevent dirt building up.*

Chainset: *Examine the alignment of your chainset regularly to ensure that the chainwheel has not been damaged.*

Lubricate: *Clean your chain regularly by spraying it with a chain cleaner and lubricant, then wiping with a cloth.*

Maintaining your bike

Toolkit: *Always carry a toolkit that contains basic equipment.*

Chain cleaner: *Run your chain through a special bath, filled with cleaner.*

Brake blocks: *Replace brake blocks when worn, as they can be hazardous.*

attachment which fits around the chain, and contains brushes and a bath which can be filled with degreaser or cleaner. Simply run the chain through a few times, and the dirt will be scrubbed off.

You should also pay attention to the chainwheels, by scrubbing with detergent and water, and also the sprockets, by removing the rear wheel and scrubbing with degreaser or detergent. Then use a rag to apply a small but consistent layer of lubricant to the chain.

Golden rules

If you keep your bike clean, and lubricate the moving parts on a regular basis, it will work more efficiently, and last much longer without breaking down. This will save you money in the long term, and also ensure that your bike remains safe to ride. Worn brakes are hazardous. Always replace worn parts before they become dangerous. A poorly maintained chain can snap, with dangerous repercussions. A well-maintained bike is a safe bike.

Above: In wet and muddy conditions, your bike builds up a lot of dirt and grease that can damage small parts.

Adjust your brakes

1 When brake blocks are worn, remove them and put new ones in, checking they are aligned with the rim.
2 If cables are stretched, replace them. Pull the cable through to the brake arms.
3 Tighten the cable. Check that the brake arms are centred. Adjust using the adjustment screw on the calliper.
4 Check that brakes are tight. If not, hold the brake blocks almost to the wheel rim, pull the cable through and tighten the bolt holding the cable.

Clean your drivetrain

1 Attach a chain bath containing degreaser to your bike, and run the chain through until the dirt has come off.
2 Remove the back wheel from your bike. Using a brush and degreaser, scrub the freewheel clean of dirt.
3 Scrub the chainwheels with detergent and water for light dirt. Use degreaser if necessary.
4 Put the back wheel in, and use a rag to apply a small but consistent layer of lubricant to the chain.

Injuries

Accidents are inevitable when you are cycling. At some point you will come off your bike or have a collision with another rider or an obstacle. There are also injuries caused by the general wear and tear that cycling inflicts on the body.

There are two major types of injuries for the typical cyclist. The first are caused by crashes. Injuries from crashes can range from a couple of scratches to, in the worst and rarest of circumstances, death. Most come somewhere in between. The second is the type of chronic injury suffered by riders through incorrect positioning or overtraining, and include bad backs and muscle strains – these tend to be less immediately painful than the first kind of injury, but they can keep you off the bike for extended periods of time.

Abrasions

For minor skin loss suffered in a crash, you can treat yourself. If you lose a lot of skin, it is a better idea to go to the hospital to get your wounds treated.

It is important, even with minor grazes and abrasions, to clean the wound thoroughly. Wounds are susceptible to infection, which can lead to illness and time off the bike. It is also important to make sure that you have had a tetanus booster in the last 10 years. If not, get one as soon as you can.

Soap and water is an adequate way of cleaning a wound, although some products are available from pharmacies to do the same job. Use a clean, sterile cloth and ensure that all the dirt is out of the wound. Once it is clean, cover it with a dressing that can be held in place with a bandage.

Broken bones

Collar bones, and to a lesser extent wrists, are susceptible to breakage in the event of a crash. When a cyclist goes down, his or her reflex is to break their fall with their hand, which can break the wrist or collarbone. If you do suffer a broken bone, you need medical attention – go to a hospital.

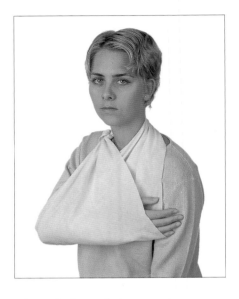

Above: Broken collarbones and arms mean extended periods off the bike. Below: Crashes are relatively common in road races – do everything you possibly can to avoid them.

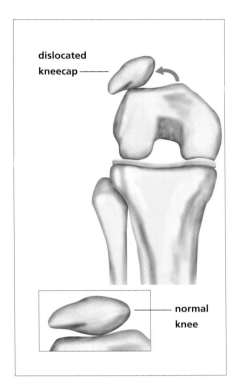

Above: The red arrow shows the direction in which the patella has dislocated. The knee joint is prone to overuse injuries – make sure your knees are aligned before pedalling.

Knee pain

All it takes is for your shoeplate to be slightly misaligned, or your saddle height to be a couple of millimetres out, or, as is more common than many people realize, your legs to be a slightly different length from each other. The repetitive nature of the cycling action will eventually exacerbate any of these problems and more, until you have chronic knee pain that prevents you from cycling.

The first thing to do when you have an injury like this is to stop cycling, which can be frustrating if you have been working hard for weeks or months. Rest, and an ice-pack on the knee, will address the immediate problem of pain and swelling. To cure the knee pain, you need to see a physiotherapist, who can assess what the root of the problem may be. Even though the pain is in your knee, the problem might be somewhere else in your body. A good physiotherapist will be able to work out why you are getting knee pain. Follow the exercise programme set for you by your physio, in order to strengthen whatever weakness is causing the knee pain, and you should be able to resume cycling within a matter of days or weeks.

Back pain

Cyclists suffer from back pain not because cycling is inherently bad for the back, but because their position or posture on the bike is putting pressure on their lower back. If your back aches during and after long rides, try to adjust your position so you are more upright, and hold the handlebars in different positions to prevent stiffness. Also, work on your core muscles to strengthen your lower back and abdomen.

Saddle sores

Cyclists spend a lot of time sitting on a narrow saddle, which puts pressure on and causes friction in their saddle area. Minute abrasions caused by the friction can become infected, leading to a saddle sore. Prevention is much better than cure. Before every ride, treat the padded insert of your shorts with antiseptic cream, and wash scrupulously after a ride. This will prevent a painful problem farther down the line.

Above: Cyclists are liable to have backache if they have bad or incorrect posture. This can lead to a curved spine.

Above: Being aware of your posture and standing up straight, can help strengthen the back and abdominal muscles.

Above: Your first aid kit should contain dressings, antiseptic wipes, bandages, scissors and adhesive tape.

Index

Credits, Acknowledgements and Resources

The publisher would like to thank the following picture libraries for the use of their pictures in the book. Every effort has been made to acknowledge the pictures properly. We apologize if there are any unintentional omissions, which will be corrected in future editions.

l=left, r=right, t=top, b=bottom, c=centre

Alamy: 56.

Andy Jones: 50t.

Corbis: 6t, 8, 14b, 20, 21, 22l, 31t, 31bl, 32t, 44 (both), 45b, 45tl, 46r, 52b, 52tc, 60tr, 68 (all), 69 (both), 70, 72t, 73bl, 73br, 75 (both), 77tc, 78, 79, 54.

Fotolibra: 9, 59tr, 61t, 66 (both), 67t, 71tr, 71bl, 71br.

Geoff Waugh: 3.3, 34, 35 (all), 58l, 80t, 83bl, 36 (both), 37 (both), 38 (both), 39 (all), 40 (both), 41 (both), 42 (all), 43 (all).

Getty: 11, 12, 15b, 60b, 71tl, 74t (Nathan Bilow/Allspor).

iStockphoto: 46l, 47l, 58r, 62bl, 62br, 64tr, 64tl, 67b, 72b, 76t.

Mike King: 31br.

Offside: 7t, 16 (both), 17 (both), 18, 19b.
Peter Drake: 63 (all).

Philip O'Connor: 1, 2, 3.1, 3.2, 3.4, 4.1, 4.2, 5.1, 5.2, 7b, 9b, 10t, 11tl, 19tr, 22r, 23 (both), 24, 25 (all), 26 (all), 27 (all), 28 (both), 29tl, 29c, 29r, 30 (both), 32b, 33t, 33c, 33br, 48 (both), 49 (all), 50bl, 50bc, 52tr, 53 (both), 59t, 59c, 59b, 64b, 77tl, 80bl, 80br, 81 (all), 82 (all), 83tl, 83tc, 83tr, 83c, 84 (both), 85 (all), 86 (all), 87 (all), 88 (all), 89 (all), 90 (all), 55 (all), 93bl.

Photolibrary: 61b.

Photoshot: 65, 73c.

Schwinn Bicycles: 15tc.

Science and Society: 10 (both).

Superstock: 33bl, 47tr, 47b, 62t, 74b, 76b, 93bc.

Wheelbase: 6b, 29b, 45tc, 45tr, 57.

The author and publishers thank the following individuals for their valuable contributions to this book and the companies who kindly supplied equipment and clothing for photography:

Evans Cycles
Hawkes BMX Club: Margaret and Scott Dick

Models for photography:
Elise Dick
Tyler Bowcombe
George Pagliero
Edward Pickering

Further reading
GENERAL
Andrews, Guy, *Road Bike Maintenance* (A&C Black, London, 2008)
Ballantine, Richard, *Richard's 21st Century Bicycle Book* (Pan, London, 2000)
Joyce, Dan, *The CTC Guide to Family Cycling* (James Pembroke Publishing, Bath, 2008)
Roberts, Tony, *Cycling: An Introduction to the Sport* (New Holland, London, 2005)
Seaton, Matt, *On Your Bike* (Black Dog Publishing, London, 2006)

TOURING
Doughty, Simon, *The Long Distance Cyclists' Handbook* (A&C Black, London, 2001)
Hughes, Tim, *Great Cycle Tours of Britain* (Ward Lock, London, 1988)
Mustoe, Anne, *A Bike Ride: 12,000 Miles Around the World* (Virgin, London, 1991)
Penn, Rob, *A Place to Cycle* (Conran Octopus, London, 2005)
Woodland, Les, *The CTC Book of Cycle Touring* (Crowood, Marlborough, 1995)

MOUNTAIN BIKING
Crowther, Nicky, *The Ultimate Mountain Bike Book* (Carlton, London, 1996)
Friel, Joe, *The Mountain Biker's Training Bible* (Velopress, Boulder, 2000)
Schmidt, Achim, *A Beginner's Guide: Mountain Biking* (Meyer and Meyer Sports Books, 2004)
Trombley, Ann, *Serious Mountain Biking* (Human Kinetics, Champaign, 2005)